THE YOUNG OXFORD LIBRARY OF SCIENCE

Atoms and Elements

David Bradley and Ian Crofton

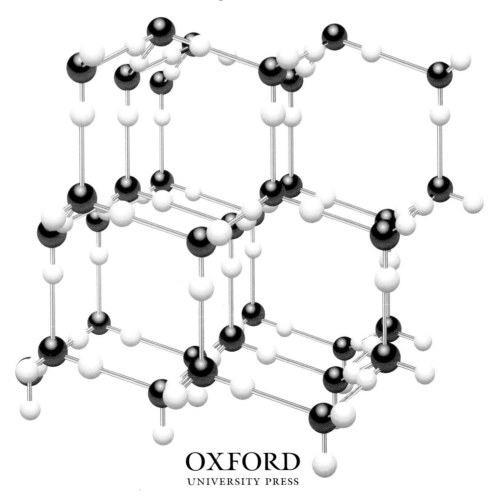

OXFORD
UNIVERSITY PRESS

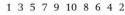

OXFORD
UNIVERSITY PRESS

Great Clarendon Street, Oxford OX2 6DP

Oxford University Press is a department of the University of Oxford.
It furthers the University's objective of excellence in research, scholarship,
and education by publishing worldwide in

Oxford New York

Auckland Bangkok Buenos Aires Cape Town Chennai
Dar es Salaam Delhi Hong Kong Istanbul Karachi
Kolkata Kuala Lumpur Madrid Melbourne Mexico City Mumbai
Nairobi São Paulo Shanghai Singapore Taipei Tokyo Toronto

with an associated company in Berlin

Oxford is a registered trade mark of Oxford University Press
in the UK and in certain other countries

British Library Cataloguing in Publication Data available

Hardback ISBN 0-19-910950-8
Paperback ISBN 0-19-910951-6

1 3 5 7 9 10 8 6 4 2

Designed and typeset by Full Steam Ahead
Printed in Malaysia.

CONTENTS

THE STUFF OF EVERYTHING

Everything around us is made of matter, from the tiniest grain of sand to the Sun in the sky. Rock, metal, wood and plastic are all made of matter. So is this book. So are you. But matter is not just solid stuff. Liquids and gases are also made of matter, so the water we drink and the air we breathe are matter as well. Scientists call solids, liquids and gases the three states of matter.

All matter is made up of tiny particles called atoms. Sometimes atoms join together to form bigger particles called molecules. Atoms and molecules are much too small to see with the naked eye.

Mass, volume and density

We work out how much matter there is in an object by measuring its mass. Mass is measured in kilograms or grams. All matter has mass. All matter also occupies space – it has volume. Volume can be measured either in cubic metres or in cubic centimetres. The volume of liquids is usually measured in litres.

Some small objects, such as a stone on a beach, have a lot of mass for their volume (their size). Some large objects, such as a hot-air balloon, have very little mass for their size. How much mass an object has

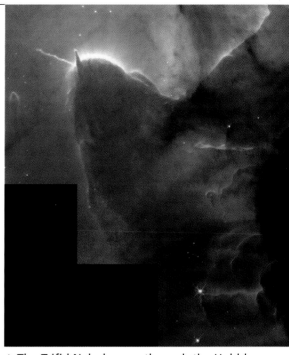

▲ The Trifid Nebula seen through the Hubble Space Telescope. Using telescopes we can see much of the matter in the Universe – planets, stars, asteroids, galaxies and nebulae. Astronomers have calculated that in outer space there is also mysterious 'dark matter' that we cannot see.

▼ The particles in any substance move around in all directions. In a solid they vibrate about a fixed point. In a liquid the particles move around more freely. In a gas they move around even more than in a liquid.

for its size is called its density. The stone has a high density, while the balloon has a low density.

The states of matter

All matter can exist in three different states: solid, liquid or gas. In nearly all substances, the solid state is the densest state, while the liquid state is less dense and the gaseous state the least dense.

Whether a substance is a solid, liquid or gas depends mainly on the temperature.

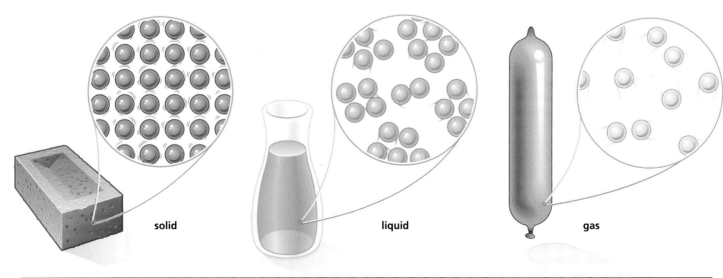

solid   liquid   gas

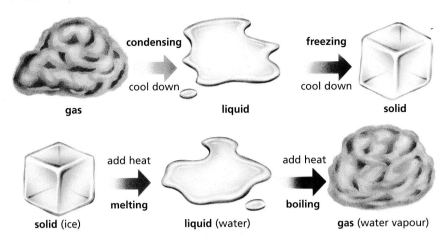

condensing
cool down
gas → liquid

freezing
cool down
→ solid

add heat
melting
solid (ice) → liquid (water)

add heat
boiling
→ gas (water vapour)

◀ Nearly all substances expand when they melt. An exception is water, which actually expands when it freezes as ice. However, like all other substances, water expands when it becomes a gas.

Most metals are normally solids, but if you heat them to a very high temperature they turn into a liquid. If you heat them even more, they turn into a gas. Substances that are gases at ordinary temperatures, such as oxygen, become liquid at very low temperatures. Oxygen becomes liquid at 183 degrees Celsius (°C) below the freezing point of water (0°C). Water itself is the only substance that is commonly found in all three states.

Changing states

Substances mainly change state because of changes in temperature. Changing from a solid to a liquid is called melting. Most substances expand when they melt. Changing from a liquid to a gas is called boiling. All substances expand when they turn into gases. Changing from a gas to a liquid is called condensing. Changing from a liquid to a solid is called freezing. Water freezes at 0°C and boils at 100°C.

When you heat a substance, you are giving it energy. When you cool it, you are taking away energy. Particles of matter (such as atoms and molecules) are always moving. They need energy to do this. How fast and freely they move depends on how much energy they have.

In a gas, the particles are free to fly around fast, like the ping-pong balls in a

key words

- boil
- condense
- density
- freeze
- gas
- liquid
- mass
- melt
- solid
- volume

▶ One of the gases present in the air around us is water vapour. As the air temperature falls in the early morning, some of this water vapour condenses (turns to liquid) as tiny drops of liquid water – dew.

lottery machine. They bump into each other and will fill every corner of a container.

If you cool a gas, its particles slow down. Eventually they become so slow that they don't bounce off each other so quickly when they hit each other. They can almost stick together, and the gas becomes a liquid.

If you cool a liquid to below its freezing point, its particles become even less energetic. The liquid becomes a solid. In a solid the particles are close together, and only move a little about fixed points.

Pressure and changing state

Pressure as well as temperature can affect whether a substance changes state. For example, the gas propane can be turned into a liquid by compressing (squeezing) it. If there is less pressure than normal, a liquid will turn into a gas more easily. For example, if you heat up water high on a Himalayan mountain where there is less air pressure than usual, the water will boil at a lower temperature. This means that it is impossible to make a good cup of tea in high mountains, because you can't get the water hot enough!

The matter in us, and in our Sun and planets, came from a huge cloud of 'stardust' – the remains of a giant star that blew up billions of years ago in a huge explosion called a supernova.

SOLID AS A ROCK

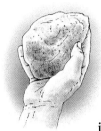

Most of the things we see around us are solids. Rocks, roads, books, pencils, computers, cars, skateboards, knives and forks – these and countless other objects are all made of solid matter. You can pick up a solid object (as long as it's not too heavy!) and turn it around.

Solids have shape and strength – unlike liquids or gases. If you tried to pick up some liquid or some gas, it would just flow away between your fingers.

key words
- amorphous
- crystalline
- matter

▼ Some solids, such as these wooden logs, are less dense than some liquids, so they float.

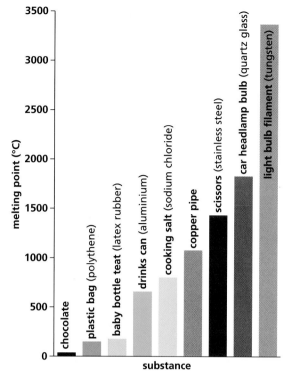

▲ Solids melt at different temperatures, depending on how strongly the atoms within them are held together.

The strength of solids

You can change the shape of some solids – you can bend, stretch, squash or twist them. But it can be hard work – all solids resist forces that try to change their shapes.

This is because the tiny particles (such as atoms) that make up a solid are held together by strong forces of attraction. The particles can only vibrate about fixed points. However, if you heat up a solid enough, the particles move about more quickly and freely – the solid melts into a liquid. Different solid materials melt at different temperatures. Butter will melt in your mouth, but iron only melts above 1500°C.

Different kinds of solids

The tiny particles that make up some kinds of solids are arranged in a regular, repeating pattern. Such solids are called crystals. Table salt, quartz and diamond are examples of solids with a crystalline structure. In other kinds of solid material the particles are arranged randomly. They are said to have an amorphous (shapeless) structure. Rubber and glass are examples of amorphous materials.

SPARKLING PATTERNS

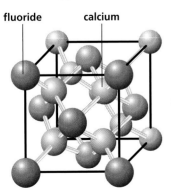

What do digital watches, diamond rings and gold ingots all have in common? They all contain crystals. A tiny piece of quartz acts as the timekeeper for digital watches, diamond is the crystal form of carbon, and all metals, except mercury, are crystalline.

All matter is made up of tiny particles (atoms or molecules). A crystal is a solid in which the particles form a regular, repeated pattern. The particles have exactly the same arrangement over and over again throughout the material. This gives a pure crystal a regular shape.

Shapes, sizes and colours

In many crystals – such as diamonds and quartz – the crystals are big and can be seen clearly. If you look at table salt through a magnifying glass, you can also see the crystalline shape. But in metals the crystals are so tiny that they can only be seen through a powerful microscope.

Crystals of table salt are shaped like tiny cubes. Other crystals form different geometrical shapes, such as pyramids, hexagons and prisms.

Lots of pure crystals, such as salt and sugar crystals, are white or transparent because all the light that hits them bounces off or travels through them. Other

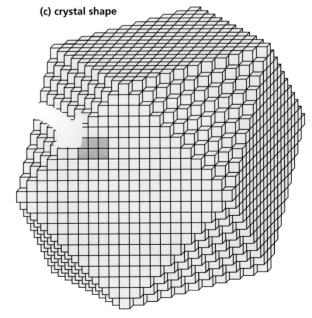

▲ These natural crystals of iron phosphate were found in Bolivia, South America.

key words
- geometrical shape
- matter
- solid

▼ Fluorite is a common mineral (a material found in rocks). Fluorite crystals have the 14-sided shape shown here (c). But the atoms in fluorite are arranged in a repeating pattern (the unit cell) that is cube-shaped (a, b).

crystals are coloured because they contain impurities. For example, both rubies and sapphires are made mostly of a material called alumina, but rubies are red because they contain tiny amounts of chromium, whereas sapphires are usually blue and contain tiny amounts of iron.

(c) crystal shape

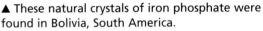

(a) unit cell

(b) 12-unit cell

fluoride   calcium

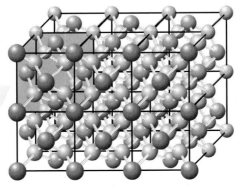

POURING MATTER

The liquid we are all most familiar with is water. All forms of life depend on water. But there are also other important liquids. For example, we use oil (in the form of petrol and diesel) to supply cars and other machines with energy, and also to help machines run smoothly. And many metal objects are made by first melting the metal, then pouring the molten liquid into a mould of the desired shape.

Unlike solids, liquids do not have a fixed shape. They can flow, and take up the shape of whatever container they are in. Liquids aren't normally as strong as solids – you can easily push your hand through a still liquid. However, unlike a gas, you cannot squeeze a liquid to make it take up less space – just try pushing a cork into a bottle that is full to the brim!

▼ A pond skater can walk on the surface of a pond because the surface of a liquid behaves like an elastic skin. The force that causes this is called surface tension. The pond skater is not heavy enough to break this 'skin'.

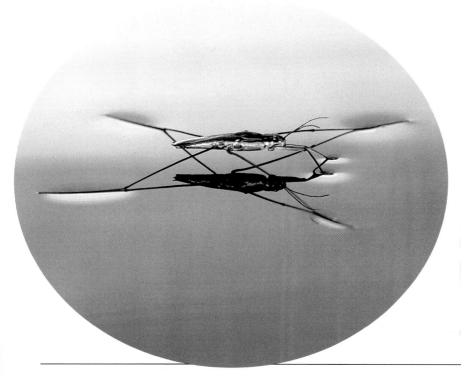

key words
- boil
- evaporate
- flow
- freeze
- surface tension
- viscosity

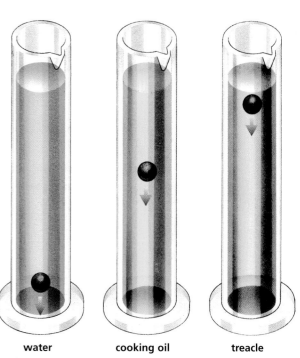

| water | cooking oil | treacle |

▲ Some liquids are thicker than others. Thicker liquids like honey or treacle flow more slowly than thinner liquids like water. Thicker liquids are said to have a higher viscosity. If you drop a ball bearing or marble into different liquids, you will see that it falls more slowly through liquids with a higher viscosity.

Particles in motion

Like all forms of matter, liquids are made up of tiny particles such as atoms and molecules. Liquids can flow and change shape because – unlike in a solid – the particles can move around each other, like marbles in a bucket.

If you cool a liquid enough, it will freeze into a solid. If you heat up a liquid, the particles move faster. Faster particles on the surface of the liquid evaporate – they escape from the surface. If you heat up the liquid more, it will boil – bubbles of gas form in the liquid, which eventually all turns into gas.

At high pressures, liquids are anything but soft. Engineers can use very fine, high-pressure jets of water to slice through metal.

THE LIQUID OF LIFE

Life on Earth would not exist without water. No plant or animal can survive without it. Two-thirds of your body is made of water. You need to drink about a litre and half of water every day to stay alive.

Water seems a simple chemical. Like many other substances, water is made up of tiny particles called molecules. Each water molecule is made up of three tinier particles called atoms. A water molecule has two atoms of hydrogen and one atom of oxygen. Scientists write this as H_2O.

Properties and uses

Water is such a common and useful chemical that scientists base the Celsius temperature scale on its freezing and boiling points. On this scale, water freezes at 0°C and boils at 100°C.

Water can dissolve lots of different chemicals, such as sugar and common salt. Because of this, chemists can use water to help make many things, from acids to medicines. Water also dissolves gases in the air, and this can cause acid rain. Where rivers pass over limestone rocks the water dissolves chemicals from the rocks. This makes the water 'hard'. It is difficult to make a good lather with soap in hard water.

We use lots of water in our homes – for washing, cleaning, cooking, drinking and flushing the lavatory. Many factories use large amounts of water to make things or to cool machinery. Hydroelectric power stations use the pressure of falling water to generate electricity.

▲ Water is one of the few substances that commonly exists as a gas, a liquid and a solid. Here, snow (ice crystals) surrounds a pool of steaming water (gas and liquid) in Yellowstone National Park, USA.

oxygen
hydrogen
single water molecule

◄ If we look at how water molecules are joined together in ice, we find that there is lots of space in the structure. This is the reason why, unlike most other substances, water actually expands when it freezes.

More than two-thirds of the Earth's surface is covered by water.

key words

- dissolve
- hard water
- ice
- steam
- water vapour

SEE-THROUGH MATTER

You may think of gases as smelly, unpleasant substances, polluting the atmosphere. Some gases are like this, but the atmosphere itself is made of air, which is a mixture of gases. We can't see or smell these gases. Air is mostly nitrogen and oxygen. We need to breathe in oxygen to live.

Liquids turn into gases when they are heated to boiling point. Water boils at 100°C. But many substances only turn into gases at very high temperatures – you need to heat molten iron to nearly 3000°C for it to boil. When you cool a gas enough, it turns into a liquid (condenses). You can also turn a gas back into a liquid by applying high pressure (squeezing it hard).

Whizzing particles

Like liquids, gases have no fixed shape and flow easily – they are fluids. But unlike liquids, gases will completely fill whatever container they are in. You can squeeze a gas to fit into a smaller container. If you put the same amount of gas into a larger container, it will expand to fill the bigger container completely.

Gases behave like this because the particles they are made of (such as atoms) are moving around very fast. This means the particles can escape the forces trying to

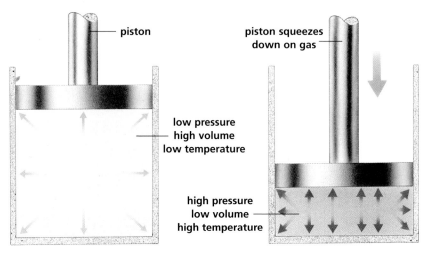

piston

piston squeezes down on gas

low pressure
high volume
low temperature

high pressure
low volume
high temperature

◀ Airships today are filled with helium gas. Helium is lighter than air and so 'floats'. Early airships used hydrogen, a gas that is also lighter than air. However, hydrogen easily catches fire, and this led to some terrible disasters.

▲ If you squeeze a gas using a piston (like in a bicycle pump), the pressure and temperature increase as the volume of the gas gets smaller.

hold them together. The particles are constantly banging into each other and against the walls of their container. This puts pressure on the walls of the container.

If you heat a gas, the particles get more energy to move even faster, and the pressure of the gas increases. If you increase the pressure of the gas by squeezing it, then the gas heats up. This is why a bicycle pump warms up when you are using it to squeeze air into your tyres.

At room temperature, the particles in air travel at around 1800 kilometres per hour – the same speed as a bullet fired from a rifle.

key words

- boiling
- fluid
- pressure

THE AIR WE BREATHE

Y ou are surrounded by gases. You can't see them, and you can't smell them. But you can feel them gently move in and out of your body as you breathe, or brush against your skin when a breeze blows.

The importance of air

For humans and other animals, the most important gas in air is oxygen. We need to breathe in oxygen to make our bodies work – without it we would die. We breathe out another gas, carbon dioxide.

Plants need carbon dioxide. They use the power of the Sun to combine carbon dioxide with water to make their own food. As they do so, they give out oxygen.

The proteins that are an essential part of our bodies are chemicals containing

The mixture of gases that surrounds us is called air. Air surrounds the whole Earth in a thick layer called the atmosphere. Air is mostly made up of nitrogen and oxygen, but there are also smaller quantities of other gases, including carbon dioxide.

◀ At sea level, the weight of air is about 1 kg for every square centimetre (100,000 pascals). As you go higher in the atmosphere, the pressure falls rapidly.

▲ If the air inside a balloon is heated, it becomes less dense (thinner) than the surrounding air and rises, lifting the balloon with it.

nitrogen. Factories can turn the nitrogen in the air into fertilizers, which help crops to grow. Unfortunately, factories and cars also release other gases into the air, which cause pollution.

Air pressure

The atmosphere extends upwards for several hundred kilometres. Although the air gets very thin high up, there is still a lot of air pressing down on us. At sea level, there is a force of about 1 kilogram pressing on every square centimetre of your body. You don't feel this pressure because your body fluids are at pressure too, and push back with the same force.

height (metres)

30,000

20,000

10,000

0

100 90 80 70 60 50 40 30 20 10 0
pressure (thousands of pascals)

● **key words**
- atmosphere
- carbon dioxide
- gases
- nitrogen
- oxygen
- pressure

MIXED-UP MATTER

In the natural world, most things are made of lots of different substances mixed up together. Rocks are mostly mixtures of minerals, usually various kinds of tiny crystals. Sand on the beach is often a mixture of tiny grains of rock and fragments of seashells. The air we breathe is a mixture of gases, mainly nitrogen and oxygen. The sea is a special kind of mixture called a solution, in which substances such as salt are dissolved.

▲ The sea is salty because it is a solution of water and various solid substances – mostly common salt (sodium chloride).

Mixtures are different from chemical compounds. For example, if you mix together iron filings and talcum powder, the mixture behaves in the same way as the two separate substances. The iron filings are still magnetic, and the talcum powder still absorbs water.

But if iron reacts chemically with oxygen in the air, a completely different chemical results – iron oxide (rust). Iron oxide is not magnetic, is reddish in colour and is much weaker than iron.

Separating mixtures

You can separate the ingredients of mixtures in various ways. Filtration is one common method. This is like passing the mixture through a sieve. If you need to separate really tiny particles from a liquid, then you need a material with even tinier holes – like filter paper. Another way of separating mixtures is to let the less dense ingredients float to the top. For example, cream floats to the top of milk, where you can skim it off.

◀ As part of the process of purifying iron and other metals, the metal is heated to melting point. The lighter impurities float to the top of the liquid and can be skimmed off as scum.

Some industrial processes use a technique called fractional distillation to separate mixtures of liquids. The liquid mixture is heated in a device called a fractionating column. Different liquids vaporize (turn to gas) at different temperatures. Those that vaporize most easily rise to the top of the column, while those with higher boiling points rise less far. This is how crude oil is refined into products such as jet fuel and petrol.

▼ Your blood is a mixture of water, cells, and various chemicals. Scientists can separate the blood cells from the liquid in a blood sample by spinning it at high speed. This forces the heavier cells to the bottom of the test tube, while the liquid is left at the top.

Solutions

Solutions are a special kind of mixture, in which one substance (the solute) is dissolved in another (the solvent). If you put sand in water and stir it up, the sand will eventually settle on the bottom. But if you stir salt into water, the salt will dissolve – it will remain evenly spread throughout the water.

Common salt is a chemical compound, sodium chloride. When a solid crystal of salt is dropped into water, molecules (tiny particles) of water gather on the surface of the crystal. They pull at the sodium and chloride particles, separating them from each other. Eventually each particle is surrounded by water molecules and the salt is dissolved.

The substances in solutions can be solids, liquids or gases. Beer and wine are solutions of two liquids – water and alcohol. Fizzy drinks are fizzy because carbon dioxide gas is dissolved in them. When you release the pressure by opening the drink, the gas fizzes out of solution.

Saturation and separation

A solvent can only dissolve a certain amount of a substance. If you go on pouring salt into a glass of water, eventually no more salt will dissolve and salt crystals will pile up at the bottom of the glass. When this happens, the solution is said to be saturated.

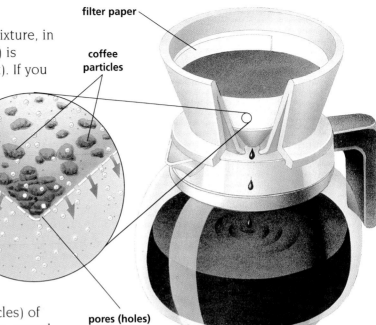

filter paper

coffee particles

pores (holes) in paper

▲ One way of making real coffee is to mix hot water and coffee grains. But if you drank it like this you would get a mouthful of gritty grains! So the mixture is separated by filter paper. This has tiny holes which are too small for the grains to get through.

You can separate a solution of salt and water by heating the solution until the water has all boiled away. You will be left with salt crystals. You can separate the water and alcohol in wine or beer by fractional distillation – alcohol boils at a lower temperature than water.

▼ How a grain of salt dissolves in water. Solid salt (sodium chloride) is made up of tiny charged particles (ions) of sodium (positively charged) and chlorine (negatively charged). Water molecules are attracted to these ions, and surround each one.

 key words
- filtration
- fractional distillation
- separation
- solute
- solvent

salt particle   chloride ion

sodium ion

water molecules

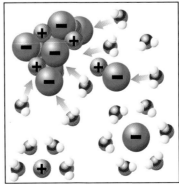

salt dissolving

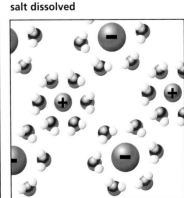

salt dissolved

THE TINIEST PARTICLES

Everything is made of atoms – from this book to your body, from trees and rocks to air and water and the planets and stars. Atoms are very tiny particles of matter – much too small to see with the naked eye. In a single drop of water, there are more than a thousand million million million atoms.

Matter is made up of different kinds of substances called elements. Oxygen, gold, iron, sulphur, carbon and hydrogen are all examples of elements. About 90 different elements occur naturally. Each element is made up of a single type of atom, and each one behaves differently.

Often atoms are joined together in larger particles called molecules. Molecules do not behave in the same way as the separate atoms. For example, the molecules of water are each made of two hydrogen atoms and one oxygen atom. Water is very different from either oxygen or hydrogen. Hydrogen is a very light gas that burns easily. Oxygen is a gas in the air we

▶ Very powerful microscopes can actually 'see' atoms. In this picture, the red, yellow and brown lumps are atoms of gold.

▼ An atom of carbon. At the centre is the nucleus, made up of protons and neutrons. Surrounding the nucleus are clouds of fast-moving electrons. The different colours of the clouds indicate different types of movement.

breathe. We cannot breathe water, or burn it! A substance such as water that is made up of the same kind of molecules is called a chemical compound.

The story of the atom

The ancient Greeks first came up with the idea of atoms. They suggested that all matter was made up of tiny particles which could not be split into any smaller pieces. In about 1803 the English scientist John Dalton described the atom as the smallest amount of an element that still behaves like that element. He realized that atoms of different elements have different weights (masses). He also showed that atoms of different elements combine together in various ways to make different chemical compounds.

Smaller and smaller

Until 1897, scientists thought there could be nothing smaller than an atom. In that year the British scientist J.J. Thomson discovered the electron. The electron has a negative electrical charge, and is much smaller than an atom. In 1911 Ernest

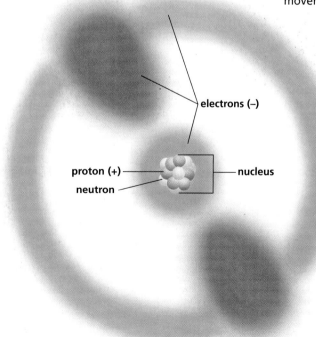

electrons (–)

proton (+)

neutron

nucleus

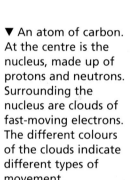

water (H₂O)

methane (CH₄)

cholesterol (C₂₇H₄₆O)

▲ Water, carbon dioxide, and natural gas (methane) are substances whose molecules are simple: they are made of only a few atoms. Cholesterol (a kind of fat in our diet) is a more complicated molecule.

Rutherford, a New Zealander living in Britain, carried out experiments with atomic particles. He concluded that atoms were mostly empty space, with a small blob of matter at the centre. He called this the nucleus. The nucleus has a positive charge, balancing the negative charge of the electrons. Rutherford thought of the electrons as flying around the nucleus like planets orbiting the Sun.

Today, scientists think of electrons as more like clouds of negative electrical charge around the nucleus. We also know

If an atom was the size of a sports stadium, then the nucleus would be the size of a housefly sitting on the grass at the centre.

▶ Scientists use enormous machines called particle accelerators to discover and find out about subatomic particles (particles smaller than atoms). This is part of the 'Main Ring' accelerator in the USA. The circular tunnel housing it is over 6 km long.

that the nucleus is made up of smaller particles called protons and neutrons. Protons have a positive electrical charge, and in an atom there are the same number of protons as electrons. Opposite electrical charges attract each other, and this attraction keeps the atom together. Scientists now think that protons and neutrons are themselves made of still smaller particles, called quarks. They have also found all kinds of other particles that are smaller than atoms.

Isotopes

Atoms of a particular element all have the same number of protons and the same number of electrons. But there may be different numbers of neutrons in different atoms, giving them different masses (weights). These different

◀ Ernest Rutherford (right) in 1908, with the equipment he later used to discover the atomic nucleus. The other man is Hans Geiger (1882–1945), who invented the Geiger counter used to measure radioactivity.

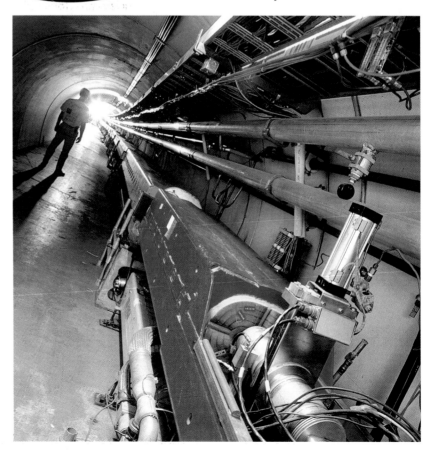

▶ By far the commonest isotope of the element carbon is carbon-12. Carbon has two other isotopes, carbon-13 and carbon-14, but these are much rarer in natural carbon.

▼ Scientists have found many ways to detect subatomic particles. This computer simulation shows the kinds of tracks made by various particles. For example, the yellow lines are the paths of particles called muons.

protons
neutrons

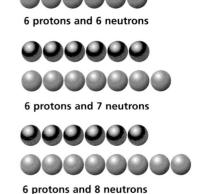

carbon-12 nucleus | 6 protons and 6 neutrons

carbon-13 nucleus | 6 protons and 7 neutrons

carbon-14 nucleus | 6 protons and 8 neutrons

Ions

In an atom, the positive electrical charges of the protons are balanced by the negative electrical charges of the electrons. The atom is therefore electrically neutral. However, if you add or take away one or more electrons from an atom, it becomes either negatively or positively charged. Such charged particles are called ions.

If you combine sodium and chlorine atoms, you can make a chemical called sodium chloride – common salt. When salt is made, the sodium atoms each give an electron to a chlorine atom. When this happens, the atoms become ions. The sodium ion has a positive charge and the chloride ion has a negative charge. The ions are attracted to each other, because opposite electrical charges attract. This is known as ionic bonding.

versions of the element are called isotopes. To identify different isotopes scientists write the total number of protons and neutrons in the isotope after the name of the element. For example, carbon-14 is an isotope of carbon with 6 protons and 8 neutrons in each atom.

Different isotopes of the same element behave in the same way in chemical reactions, but they may have different physical properties. For example, carbon-14 is radioactive, but carbon-12 is not. However, both isotopes can combine with oxygen chemically to make the compound carbon dioxide. Most elements found in nature are a mixture of different isotopes.

 key words
- compound
- electron
- element
- neutron
- nucleus
- proton

▼ Ions with opposite charges (+ and –) are attracted to each other.

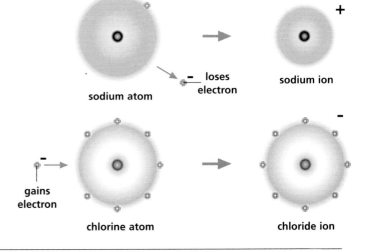

sodium atom | loses electron | sodium ion +

gains electron | chlorine atom | chloride ion –

INVISIBLE DANGER

In 1945, near the end of World War II, an atomic bomb was dropped on the Japanese city of Hiroshima. Some 80,000 people died in the terrible explosion. But many more died later from an invisible danger – the radioactivity produced as the bombs exploded. The radioactivity caused all kinds of diseases, including cancers that only appeared many years later.

Radioactivity is what happens when the atoms of certain unstable elements, such as the heavy metal uranium, break down to atoms of more stable elements. As they do this, they give off radiation.

Types of radiation

When radioactive materials break down, they send out tiny particles, smaller than atoms. These are called alpha particles and beta particles. They also send out gamma rays, which are a kind of wave, like light waves but carrying much more energy.

▶ Marie Curie (1867–1934) worked with her husband Pierre (1859–1906) on the study of radioactivity. They won the Nobel Prize in 1903 for their discovery of the radioactive elements polonium and radium. Marie died of a disease caused by radioactivity.

All forms of radioactivity can be dangerous, but some are more penetrating than others. Paper can block alpha particles, but only a sheet of light metal will stop beta particles. To block gamma rays you need a thick sheet of lead. Doctors use small doses of gamma rays to destroy some kinds of cancer.

Dangers and uses

Nuclear power stations produce lots of dangerous radioactivity, but this is carefully contained behind thick walls, and radioactive waste is buried deep underground. Lots of natural materials are slightly radioactive, but mostly not enough to be harmful. For example, plants and animals take in small amounts of radioactive carbon from the atmosphere. Radioactive materials break down at regular rates, so archaeologists can tell how old many things are by measuring the amount of radioactive carbon that is left in them.

Scientists use radioactive substances in other kinds of research. For example, they can trace the passage of a harmless radioactive substance through the body using a Geiger counter, a device that detects radioactivity.

Type of radiation	Type of atom	Half-life
α	uranium-238	4.5×10^9 years
β	thorium-234	24.5 days
β	protactinium-234	1.14 minutes
α	uranium-234	2.33×10^5 years
α	thorium-230	8.3×10^4 years
α	radium-226	1590 years
α	radon-222	3.825 days
α	polonium-218	3.5 minutes
β	lead-214	26.8 minutes
β	bismuth-214	19.7 minutes
α	polonium-214	1.5×10^{-4} seconds
β	lead-210	22 years
β	bismuth-210	5 days
α	polonium-210	140 days
	lead-206	stable

◀ Natural uranium slowly breaks down over billions of years to the metal lead. As it breaks down, it gives off radioactivity in the form of harmful alpha (α) and beta (β) particles. Each stage in the process has a different half-life (the time taken for half the material to break down).

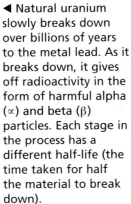

key words

- alpha particle
- beta particle
- gamma ray
- radioactive material
- radioactivity

ENERGY FROM ATOMS

Atoms are the tiny particles from which all matter is made. They are so small that 4000 million of them would fit across the full stop at the end of this sentence. Yet vast amounts of energy are locked up in every atom. Scientists have used this energy to make bombs with awesomely destructive powers. More peacefully, this energy is used to produce electricity, or to power ships and submarines.

The tiny particle at the centre of every atom is called the nucleus. It is made up of smaller particles called protons and neutrons. We call the energy we tap from atoms nuclear energy because it comes from the nucleus of the atom.

Splitting atoms

The most common substance used to produce nuclear energy is a heavy metal called uranium. It gives out energy when its atoms split. This process is a kind of nuclear reaction, called fission. Nuclear fission releases vast amounts of energy – much more than in any chemical reactions, even fire or explosions. One kilogram of uranium fuel can produce the same amount of energy as 55,000 kilograms (55 tonnes) of coal.

Scientists first used nuclear energy to make atomic bombs, like the ones dropped on Japan in 1945 at the end of World War II. Before that, the biggest bombs contained less than half a tonne of ordinary explosives. The first atomic bomb dropped on Japan exploded with the force of 20,000 tonnes of ordinary explosives.

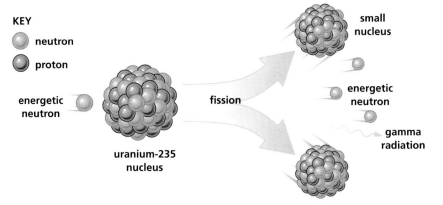

KEY
- neutron
- proton

energetic neutron

uranium-235 nucleus

fission

small nucleus

energetic neutron

gamma radiation

▲ In the fission of uranium, a neutron hits the nucleus of a uranium atom and splits it in two. Several neutrons are released, along with enormous amounts of energy. Each neutron released from the fission reaction can go on to split other uranium nuclei in a chain reaction, releasing more and more energy.

In the years that followed World War II scientists worked to use nuclear energy for peaceful purposes. The first nuclear power station – Calder Hall, Cumbria, UK – started to produce electricity in 1956.

The nuclear reactor

The main part of a nuclear power station is the reactor. The nuclear 'fuel', uranium, is packed into the centre, or core, of the reactor. This is where nuclear fission takes place. A coolant (cooling substance) passes through the core and carries away the heat produced by fission. It is led away to produce steam. The steam is used to drive turbines that generate electricity.

◀ A US Navy Trident missile is launched from the nuclear-powered submarine Ohio during practice manoeuvres off the coast of Florida. Trident missiles are designed to carry a nuclear warhead that explodes with the power of 100,000 tonnes of TNT (a conventional explosive).

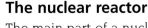 **key words**
- atom
- fission
- fusion
- nuclear reaction
- nucleus
- reactor

The reactor is controlled by control rods. These are pulled out or pushed in to make the nuclear reaction go faster or slower. If something goes wrong, the rods are automatically pushed right in to shut the reactor down.

Radiation danger

Nuclear power stations are 'cleaner' than ordinary power stations burning oil, gas or coal to produce steam, because nuclear power stations do not produce gases that pollute the air. But not many new ones are being built, beacause they suffer from a serious drawback. Uranium fuel and substances produced in nuclear reactors are radioactive – they give off penetrating radiation that is dangerous to living things.

For this reason, nuclear reactors are built with thick steel and concrete walls to stop the radiation escaping. But this isn't the end of the problem. Nuclear reactors produce dangerous radioactive waste, which could harm people, animals and the environment. Some of the waste will have to be stored for thousands of years before it becomes safe. It is often buried deep underground, embedded in glass blocks.

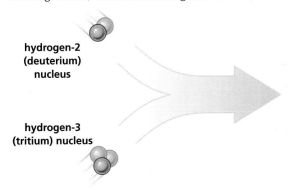

hydrogen-2 (deuterium) nucleus

hydrogen-3 (tritium) nucleus

neutron

helium-4 nucleus

KEY

neutron

proton

Powering the Sun and the stars

Nearly all life on Earth depends on heat and light energy from the Sun. The energy that powers the Sun and the other stars, making them shine, comes from a different kind of nuclear reaction called fusion. In nuclear fusion, energy is not produced when atomic nuclei split, but when they join together (fuse). In the commonest fusion process, pairs of hydrogen atoms fuse together to form atoms of another element – helium.

▼ In nuclear fusion, two special hydrogen atoms are joined to make an atom of helium. One neutron is released, plus even more energy than in nuclear fission. The hydrogen atoms used in fusion are deuterium (1 proton and 1 neutron) and tritium (1 proton and 2 neutrons).

▶ A scientist takes a dead fish from a lake near Chernobyl, in Ukraine. In 1986 there was a serious accident at the nuclear power station there. Radioactive material escaped and spread over a vast area.

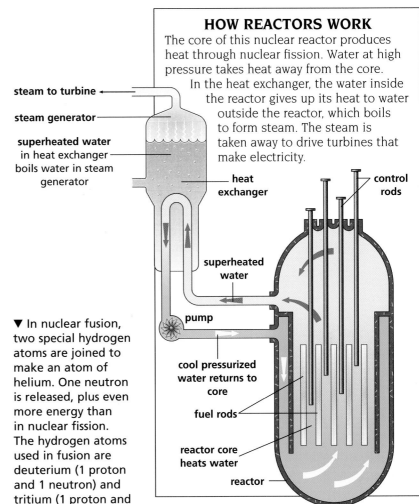

HOW REACTORS WORK

The core of this nuclear reactor produces heat through nuclear fission. Water at high pressure takes heat away from the core. In the heat exchanger, the water inside the reactor gives up its heat to water outside the reactor, which boils to form steam. The steam is taken away to drive turbines that make electricity.

steam to turbine

steam generator

superheated water in heat exchanger boils water in steam generator

heat exchanger

control rods

superheated water

pump

cool pressurized water returns to core

fuel rods

reactor core heats water

reactor

Scientists have already used nuclear fusion on Earth to make bombs – hydrogen bombs. Hydrogen bombs explode with the force of tens of millions of tonnes of ordinary explosives. Unfortunately, scientists have not yet managed to control nuclear fusion to produce power for peaceful uses.

NATURE'S BUILDING BLOCKS

In the ancient world people believed that all things were made from mixtures of four basic substances – earth, water, air and fire. We know now that this is not true. All things are made of basic substances, which are called elements. About 90 different elements are found in nature. But earth, water, air and fire are not among them.

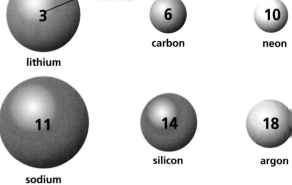

lithium

3 ← atomic number

6 carbon

10 neon

11 sodium

14 silicon

18 argon

▲ The atoms in an element are all the same, but the atoms of different elements are different sizes. Heavier atoms (ones having more protons and electrons) are not always bigger than lighter ones. The elements shown here are in order of increasing atomic number (number of protons).

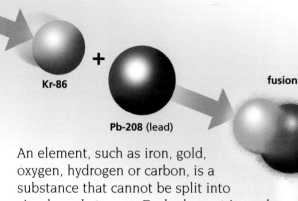

Kr-86 + Pb-208 (lead)

fusion

An element, such as iron, gold, oxygen, hydrogen or carbon, is a substance that cannot be split into simpler substances. Each element is made up of tiny identical particles called atoms. Each element has a unique size of atom that behaves in a particular way.

Atoms of different elements can combine together to form larger particles called molecules. Chemical compounds are substances made of molecules that contain atoms of different elements. For example, a molecule of methane (natural gas) is made from an atom of carbon and four atoms of hydrogen.

◀ Recently, scientists tried to make a new element – ununoctium, or element 118. They did this by bombarding lead atoms with krypton atoms, but the new atoms they claimed to have produced broke up almost immediately.

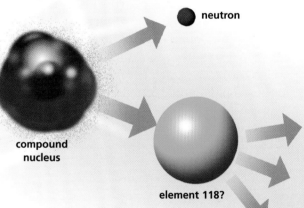

neutron

compound nucleus

element 118?

▼ Most elements exist in nature as parts of mixtures or compounds. However, gold is often found in its pure form.

All kinds of elements

Although only about 90 elements exist naturally, scientists have made around 25 new elements in nuclear reactors and scientific laboratories. Many of these 'artificial' elements are very unstable and only exist for fractions of a second.

At room temperature most elements are solids, but a number are gases (for example, oxygen, hydrogen, nitrogen, helium and neon). Only two are liquids – mercury and bromine. Most elements are metals – only 19 are non-metals (for example, carbon, sulphur and iodine). A further 5 are metalloids – elements such as silicon that are half-way between metals and non-metals.

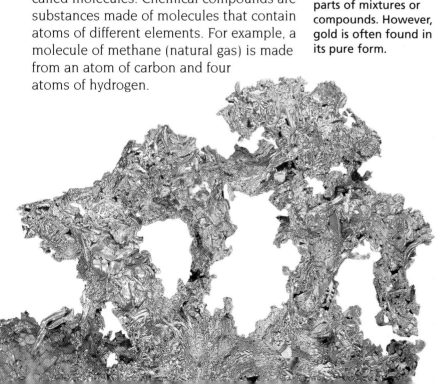

Quite a number of the heavier elements are radioactive (they give off radiation). Some elements, such as gold, rarely combine with others to make chemical compounds. Others, such as fluorine, are highly reactive.

Some elements exist in different forms, called allotropes. For instance, diamonds and graphite are allotropes of carbon.

Millions of compounds

While there are fewer than 120 elements, scientists have found or made more than 26 million different compounds – most of them in the last 70 years or so.

Some compounds are very simple. Water consists of molecules containing two hydrogen atoms and one oxygen atom. Scientists write this as H_2O. Other compounds are more complicated. For example, the common drug aspirin contains 21 atoms, and is written by scientists as $CH_3COOC_6H_4COOH$ (C stands for a carbon atom, H for a hydrogen atom and O for an oxygen atom). The molecules of some compounds – like the enzymes in your stomach that help you digest your food – each contain thousands of atoms.

Compounds do not behave in the same way as the elements they are made of. You can sprinkle a little sodium chloride (table salt) on your food without coming to any

▶ The Greek philosopher Aristotle (384–322 BC) first suggested that everything was made of four basic substances or elements: earth (*terra*), water (*aqua*), air (*aeris*) and fire (*ignis*). This belief lasted for 2000 years. It became mixed up with all kinds of mystical and magical ideas – as you can see in this early 17th-century engraving featuring the astrological signs of the zodiac.

harm. However, pure sodium would burn a hole in your tongue, and pure chlorine is a gas that would poison you.

The way a compound behaves also depends on how many atoms of a particular element are in each of its molecules. For example, you breathe in the small amounts of carbon dioxide (CO_2) in the atmosphere all the time. In contrast, carbon monoxide (CO) is a highly poisonous gas.

key words
- allotrope
- atom
- bond
- molecule

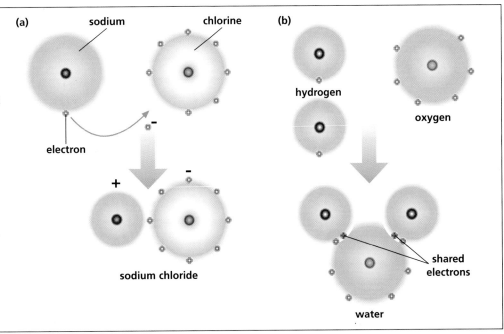

CHEMICAL BONDS

The molecules in chemical compounds are held together by bonds between the atoms.

In some kinds of compound, bonds are made when one atom gives at least one electron to another atom. This is called an ionic bond. In example (a), sodium gives an electron to chlorine to form sodium chloride (salt).

In other kinds of compound the atoms share at least one pair of electrons, one from each atom. This is called a covalent bond. Water (b) is a covalent compound, in which oxygen shares electrons with two hydrogen atoms.

(a) sodium   chlorine   (b)

hydrogen   oxygen

electron

sodium chloride

hydrogen

shared electrons

water

ORDERING THE ELEMENTS

Elements are the basic substances that everything on the Earth and in the Universe is made of – including us. Your body is mostly made of the elements carbon, hydrogen, and oxygen. Elements cannot be split into simpler substances. About 90 different elements are found in nature, and scientists have managed to make several more.

Although each element is different, some elements behave in a similar way to other elements. In the 19th century, chemists struggled to discover a pattern in the 60 or so elements then known. Then, towards the end of the century, the Russian chemist

CREATED IN A DREAM

The French chemist Antoine Lavoisier (1743–1794) knew about 33 elements. He tried to arrange them in a table in 1789. He classified the gases, metals, non-metals and earth elements. By the time of the Russian chemist Dmitri Mendeleev (1834–1907), 65

Dmitri Mendeleev

elements were known. Mendeleev is said to have had the idea for organizing elements into a periodic table in a dream. He realized that there were gaps in his table, and even predicted the chemical properties of these missing elements.

Dmitri Mendeleev found a pattern. This pattern, which is still used today, is called the periodic table.

Using this table, Mendeleev predicted that certain unknown elements would be discovered to fill the gaps in the table. When these elements were later discovered, scientists found they behaved as Mendeleev had predicted they would.

▼ The periodic table of the elements.

element name — chromium
atomic number — 24
chemical symbol — **Cr**
atomic mass (weight) — 51.996

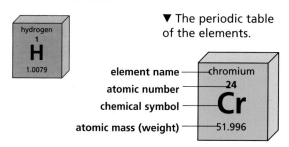

hydrogen 1 **H** 1.0079											
lithium 3 **Li** 6.941	berylium 4 **Be** 9.0122										
sodium 11 **Na** 22.990	magnesium 12 **Mg** 24.305										
potassium 19 **K** 39.098	calcium 20 **Ca** 40.078	scandium 21 **Sc** 44.956	titanium 22 **Ti** 47.867	vandium 23 **V** 50.942	chromium 24 **Cr** 51.996	manganese 25 **Mn** 54.938	iron 26 **Fe** 55.845	cobalt 27 **Co** 58.933	nickel 28 **Ni** 58.693	copper 29 **Cu** 63.546	zinc 30 **Zn** 65.39
rubidium 37 **Rb** 85.468	strontium 38 **Sr** 87.62	yttrium 39 **Y** 88.906	zirconium 40 **Zr** 91.224	niobium 41 **Nb** 92.906	molybdenum 42 **Mo** 95.94	technetium 43 **Tc** (97.907)	ruthenium 44 **Ru** 101.07	rhodium 45 **Rh** 102.91	palladium 46 **Pd** 106.42	silver 47 **Ag** 107.87	cadmium 48 **Cd** 112.41
caesium 55 **Cs** 132.91	barium 56 **Ba** 137.33	lutetium 71 **Lu** 174.97	hafnium 72 **Hf** 178.49	tantaium 73 **Ta** 180.95	tungsten 74 **W** 183.84	rhenium 75 **Re** 186.21	osmium 76 **Os** 190.23	iridium 77 **Ir** 192.22	platinum 78 **Pt** 195.08	gold 79 **Au** 196.97	mercury 80 **Hg** 200.59
francium 87 **Fr** (223.02)	radium 88 **Ra** (226.03)	lawrencium 103 **Lr** (262.11)	rutherfordium 104 **Rf** (263.11)	dubnium 105 **Db** (262.11)	seaborgium 106 **Sg** (266.12)	bohrium 107 **Bh** (264.12)	hassium 108 **Hs** (269.13)	meitnerium 109 **Mt** (268.14)	ununnilium 110 **Uun** (272.15)	unununium 111 **Uuu** (272.15)	ununbium 112 **Uub** (277)

lanthanum 57 **La** 138.91	cerium 58 **Ce** 140.12	praseodymium 59 **Pr** 140.91	neodymium 60 **Nd** 144.24	promethium 61 **Pm** (144.91)	samarium 62 **Sm** 150.36	europium 63 **Eu** 151.96	gadolinium 64 **Gd** 157.25	terbium 65 **Tb** 158.93	dysprosium 66 **Dy** 162.50	holmium 67 **Ho** 164.93	erbium 68 **Er** 167.26	thulium 69 **Tm** 168.93	ytterbium 70 **Yb** 173.04
actinium 89 **Ac** (227.03)	thorium 90 **Th** 232.04	protactinium 91 **Pa** 231.04	uranium 92 **U** 238.03	neptunium 93 **Np** (237.05)	plutonium 94 **Pu** (244.06)	americium 95 **Am** (243.06)	curium 96 **Cm** (247.07)	berkelium 97 **Bk** (247.07)	californium 98 **Cf** (251.08)	einsteinium 99 **Es** (252.08)	fermium 100 **Fm** (257.10)	mendelevium 101 **Md** (258.10)	nobelium 102 **No** (259.10)

Different kinds of atom

All the elements are made up of tiny particles called atoms. Mendeleev knew that different elements had atoms with different weights. Scientists now know that the atoms of different elements also have different structures.

The small particle at the centre (nucleus) of an atom contains even smaller particles called protons and neutrons. Other tiny particles called electrons whizz round the nucleus. In any atom there are the same number of electrons and protons.

Each element has a different size of atom. The atomic number in the periodic table tells you how many protons there are in an atom of the element. The electrons are arranged in 'shells' around the nucleus. The way an element behaves depends on how many electrons there are in the outermost shell.

Understanding the periodic table

The periodic table is set out in groups (the columns going up and down) and periods (the rows going across the table). All the elements in a group behave in a similar way. For example, the column on the far left is the group of the most reactive metals. The group includes sodium (atomic number 11) and potassium (19), which react violently if put in water, whereas rubidium (37) is even more reactive, bursting into flames if exposed to air. In complete contrast, the column on the far right is the group of noble gases – the elements that are least reactive. The group includes several gases, such as helium (2) and neon (10), that are found in small quantities in the air we breathe.

If you look across the table from left to right, each period (row) starts with a so-called alkali metal, followed by an alkaline earth metal. For example, in the third period sodium (Na) is an alkali metal, while magnesium (Mg) is an alkaline earth metal.

There are many more metals than non-metals in the periodic table. Many of the commonest metals, such as iron and copper, fall in a large block known as the transition metals (coloured green in the diagram). The non-metals fall to the right of a ziz-zag dividing line (coloured blue in the diagram). Among the non-metals, the last but one column is a group of highly reactive elements called the halogens. The halogen in period 3 is chlorine (Cl). Next to chlorine, in the far-right column, is the unreactive noble gas argon (Ar).

There have been hundreds of attempts to improve on the Mendeleev-style periodic table, including three-dimensional and circular tables. None of them have displaced the 'long-form' that we use today, which was based on Mendeleev's first table.

Earth
Cold and dry.

Water
Cold and wet.

Air
Hot and wet.

Fire
Hot and dry.

▲ Old symbols for various 'elements' (air, fire, earth and water were thought to be elements, but we know now that this is not the case). In the Middle Ages, people called alchemists tried to turn metals such as lead into gold. They made several important chemical discoveries during their experiments.

helium 2 **He** 4.0026

boron 5 **B** 10.811	carbon 6 **C** 12.011	nitrogen 7 **N** 14.007	oxygen 8 **O** 15.999	fluorine 9 **F** 18.998	neon 10 **Ne** 20.180
aluminium 13 **Al** 26.982	silicon 14 **Si** 28.086	phosphorus 15 **P** 30.974	sulphur 16 **S** 32.066	chlorine 17 **Cl** 35.453	argon 18 **Ar** 39.948
gallium 31 **Ga** 69.723	germanium 32 **Ge** 72.61	arsenic 33 **As** 74.922	selenium 34 **Se** 78.96	bromine 35 **Br** 79.904	krypton 36 **Kr** 83.80
indium 49 **In** 114.82	tin 50 **Sn** 118.71	antimony 51 **Sb** 121.76	tellurium 52 **Te** 127.60	iodine 53 **I** 126.90	xenon 54 **Xe** 131.29
thallium 81 **Tl** 204.38	lead 82 **Pb** 207.2	bismuth 83 **Bi** 208.98	polonium 84 **Po** (208.98)	astatine 85 **At** (209.99)	radon 86 **Rn** (222.02)
ununquadium 114 **Uuq** (289)		ununhexium 116 **Uuh** (289)		ununoctium 118 **Uuo** (293)	

key words

- atom
- atomic number
- element
- group
- period
- periodic table

DIVIDING THE ELEMENTS

For some two million years, early humans used tools made of stone. Then, about 5000 years ago, people discovered how to extract metal from rocks and to make metal tools. To begin with, people used copper and bronze (an alloy, or mixture, of copper and tin). Then came iron, and finally steel.

Most of the elements – the substances from which all things are made – are metals. Metals have many properties in common, but non-metals have a wide variety of properties. Several of the non-metals, such as carbon and oxygen, are present in large quantities in living things. But our bodies need only tiny amounts of metals such as iron and zinc.

▶ Mercury is the only metal that is a liquid at room temperature.

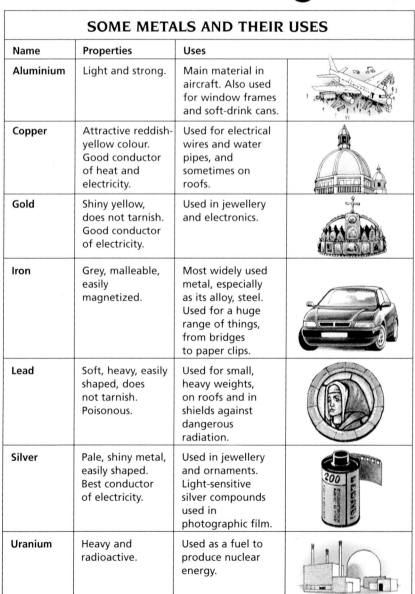

▼ Steel is very strong for its weight. It is the main structural material in the London Eye, a 135-metre tall ferris wheel in London, UK.

SOME METALS AND THEIR USES

Name	Properties	Uses	
Aluminium	Light and strong.	Main material in aircraft. Also used for window frames and soft-drink cans.	
Copper	Attractive reddish-yellow colour. Good conductor of heat and electricity.	Used for electrical wires and water pipes, and sometimes on roofs.	
Gold	Shiny yellow, does not tarnish. Good conductor of electricity.	Used in jewellery and electronics.	
Iron	Grey, malleable, easily magnetized.	Most widely used metal, especially as its alloy, steel. Used for a huge range of things, from bridges to paper clips.	
Lead	Soft, heavy, easily shaped, does not tarnish. Poisonous.	Used for small, heavy weights, on roofs and in shields against dangerous radiation.	
Silver	Pale, shiny metal, easily shaped. Best conductor of electricity.	Used in jewellery and ornaments. Light-sensitive silver compounds used in photographic film.	
Uranium	Heavy and radioactive.	Used as a fuel to produce nuclear energy.	

Properties of metals

All the metals (apart from mercury) are solids at room temperature. They all have a crystalline structure, although the crystals are much too small to see with the naked eye. Pure metals are shiny when polished. Metals are good conductors of electricity and heat. Many of them are quite strong – you can squeeze them or stretch them and they won't break. But metals are malleable – you can shape them by hammering or rolling them. Many are also ductile – you can draw them out into thin wires.

Despite these similarities, there are differences among the metals. Metals such as tin, lead and aluminium, are softer, weaker and melt at lower temperatures than metals such as iron and copper.

▶ Metals are generally good conductors of electricity. Many non-metals do not conduct electricity well, and non-metallic materials such as ceramics, glass, plastics and rubber are used as insulators – like the glass insulators on these high-voltage cables.

key words

- allotrope
- alloy
- conductor
- crystal
- ductile
- malleable

SOME NON-METALS AND THEIR USES

Name	Properties	Uses	
Carbon	Exists as diamond, graphite or soot.	All forms of life on Earth are based on carbon compounds.	
Chlorine	Greenish, poisonous gas. Highly reactive.	Used to disinfect swimming pools and drinking water. Compounds include table salt.	
Helium	Very light, non-reactive gas.	Used to fill airships, and in the air breathed by divers.	
Hydrogen	The lightest element. A gas in its pure form.	Huge numbers of important compounds, including water and most of the chemicals that make up living things.	
Neon	Invisible, unreactive gas.	Used in strip lighting.	
Nitrogen	Invisible gas.	The main gas in air. Compounds important in all living things, and in fertilizers.	
Oxygen	Invisible gas.	Essential to respiration (breathing), and to combustion (burning).	
Phosphorus	White, red or black solid.	Used in matches. Some compounds found in living things, and others used as fertilizers.	
Sulphur	Exists as various kinds of yellow solid.	Used in matches, gunpowder and in vulcanizing (strengthening) rubber. Many important compounds.	

Some metals, such as sodium and potassium, are highly reactive, while others, like gold and platinum, are unreactive.

Gold is one of the few elements that is found in its pure state in nature. Many other metals are only found in minerals in rocks, where they are combined with non-metals. For example, the main iron minerals are compounds of iron and oxygen.

Metals can be made stronger by melting them together to make alloys. Steel is an alloy of iron and carbon (a non-metal). Stainless steel contains the metals chromium and nickel.

Properties of non-metals

Some of the non-metallic elements are also very reactive – especially the halogens, such as chlorine. Other non-metals, the noble gases such as helium, are the least reactive of all the elements.

The non-metals include gases such as oxygen and nitrogen, solids such as carbon and sulphur, and one liquid, bromine. Some solid non-metals can have different forms, called allotropes. The allotropes of carbon include diamond and graphite. Non-metals are generally poor conductors of electricity, although graphite is an exception.

The metalloids

A few elements have properties in between metals and non-metals. These are the metalloids. The metalloids silicon and germanium are semiconductors – they can be treated with chemicals to change how well they conduct electricity. Semiconductors are important in electronics.

THE LIGHTEST GAS

Hydrogen is the lightest of all the elements (the substances from which all matter is made). It is also the commonest element in the Universe. It is found in everything, from the stars and galaxies in space to the water you drink and the food you eat, and every part of your body.

Hydrogen in its pure form is a non-poisonous gas. You cannot see, smell or taste it. On the Earth hydrogen is rarely found on its own. When mixed with oxygen in the atmosphere it forms a highly explosive mixture that ignites with a single spark. In this process, the hydrogen combines with the oxygen to form water – water molecules have two atoms of hydrogen and one atom of oxygen.

▶ Hydrogen is a powerful fuel. The main engines of the Space Shuttle are powered by hydrogen.

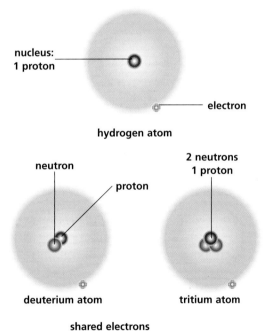

nucleus: 1 proton

electron

hydrogen atom

neutron

proton

2 neutrons 1 proton

deuterium atom

tritium atom

shared electrons

hydrogen molecule

◀ Hydrogen is so light because its atoms have only one proton and one electron. However, there are some kinds of hydrogen (deuterium and tritium) that are heavier. These types are used to make hydrogen bombs. Hydrogen gas is made up of molecules, each containing two hydrogen atoms.

key words

- compound
- element
- hydrogen
- proton

Hydrogen compounds

Hydrogen combines with other elements in numerous ways, making millions of different chemical substances. In food it is present in carbohydrates, vitamins, proteins and fats. Nearly every chemical from which your body is made contains hydrogen. And our most important fuels – coal, oil and natural gas – are compounds made up mainly of carbon and hydrogen.

Uses of hydrogen

Industry gets most of its hydrogen from natural gas. Hydrogen is used to make farm fertilizers, margarine and plastics.

Because it is so light, hydrogen was once used to fill airships. But in the 1930s there were some terrible accidents when airships caught fire. Airships now use helium gas, which does not burn. The fact that hydrogen does burn so explosively, however, makes it a good fuel for space rockets. In the future it may also be used to fuel cars and trucks – the only exhaust fumes would be water vapour!

THE ELEMENT OF LIFE

What links a clear, sparkling diamond and the dirty black soot inside a chimney? Amazingly, although they look so different, they are both made of pure carbon. Perhaps even more amazingly, all known forms of life – from microscopic bacteria to human beings – are mainly made up of substances containing carbon. Carbon is the element of life.

Pure carbon exists in several different forms, including diamond, soot and graphite (the material used for the 'lead' in your pencil). Carbon also combines with many other elements, making millions of different chemical compounds.

▶ Animals, such as the wolf shown here, use oxygen in their bodies, and produce carbon dioxide as a waste product. The air that animals breathe out is rich in carbon dioxide. (You can't actually see the carbon dioxide: what you see here is the moisture in the wolf's breath.)

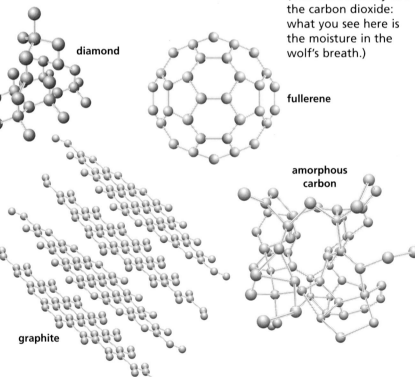

diamond

fullerene

amorphous carbon

graphite

▲ Pure carbon takes different forms because of the different ways that carbon atoms fit together. Fullerenes come in various shapes and sizes. In the 'buckyball', there are 60 atoms fitted together in 20 hexagons and 12 pentagons. Soot is an example of amorphous carbon, in which the atoms do not make a regular shape.

● **key words**
- allotrope
- amorphous
- carbon cycle
- diamond
- fullerene
- graphite

Forms and uses of pure carbon

Different forms of the same element are called allotropes. Carbon has several allotropes. Diamond is a crystalline form of carbon. It is the hardest material known. This hardness makes it excellent for cutting tools as well as for jewellery.

Another allotrope, graphite, has a different crystalline structure. It is grey or black, and is soft and flaky. It feels greasy when you touch it, and is used as a lubricant (a substance that helps machines run smoothly). It is also used for pencil leads and as a pigment (colouring) in inks used for printing. It also conducts electricity and is used, for example, in batteries. It has a very high melting point, and so containers made of graphite are used to hold molten metals.

The carbon you find in soot, charcoal and burnt toast is amorphous ('shapeless') carbon – the carbon atoms do not form a regular shape. Specially treated charcoal is used in gas masks and for absorbing unpleasant smells.

Coal is mostly carbon, and is built out of rings and chains of carbon atoms. Coke – which is made from coal – has an even higher amount of carbon. The carbon from coke is added to iron to make steel, which is a much stronger metal. The fullerenes are the most recently discovered allotrope of carbon. The atoms in fullerenes form molecules with shapes like soccer and rugby balls as well as tubes.

Carbon compounds

A carbon atom can have up to four other atoms joined to it at a time. Carbon atoms can join up with other carbon atoms to make rings and chains. They can also join with almost every other element – from hydrogen to tungsten – to make a huge number of different compounds.

One of the simplest and most important compounds of carbon is carbon dioxide. This gas is formed when your body takes energy from food – the carbon in the food combines with the oxygen you breathe in from the air. You then breathe out carbon dioxide. Carbon dioxide from the atmosphere is essential to plants, which use it to make their own food.

When carbon combines with hydrogen, it forms a group of materials called hydrocarbons. Crude oil and natural gas are made mostly from hydrocarbons. When they are burnt, carbon dioxide is released into the atmosphere.

When carbon combines with oxygen and hydrogen it forms carbohydrates – foods like sugar and starch. Plants make carbohydrates from carbon dioxide and water, and we get carbohydrates from plants.

When carbon combines with nitrogen as well as oxygen and hydrogen, it can make

very complicated chemicals called proteins. Proteins are among the most important substances that make up living things.

The compounds of carbon that contain hydrogen, or carbon and hydrogen and any other element, are called organic compounds. This is because chemists once thought they were formed only by living things. However, chemists can now make millions of different organic compounds in the laboratory.

THE CARBON CYCLE

In the natural world, carbon is used again and again in a process called the carbon cycle. Plants take in carbon dioxide from the air to make their own food. Carbon is transferred to animals when they eat the plants, or eat other animals that eat plants. Animals release carbon back into the air in the form of carbon dioxide when they breathe out. When animals and plants die they decompose (rot). Over millions of years the remains of plants and animals can form fossil fuels. When we burn fossil fuels as a source of energy, carbon is returned to the air in the form of carbon dioxide.

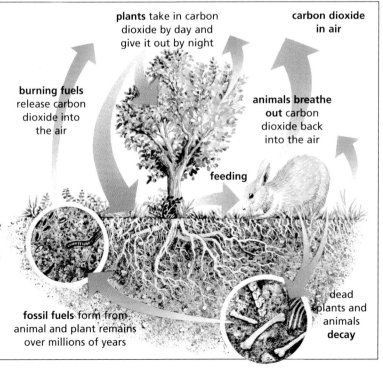

plants take in carbon dioxide by day and give it out by night

carbon dioxide in air

burning fuels release carbon dioxide into the air

animals breathe out carbon dioxide back into the air

feeding

fossil fuels form from animal and plant remains over millions of years

dead plants and animals decay

▲ Carbon fibre is made by heating textile fibres. The carbon fibres are only a few thousandths of a millimetre across. They can be squashed together to make tough, flexible materials. These are used for making many things, from tennis rackets to the racing yacht shown here.

ATMOSPHERIC GAS

When you breathe, most of the air that enters your lungs is nitrogen. Only about one-fifth of the air is oxygen. Your body doesn't use the nitrogen you breathe in. You just breathe it out again. However, much of your body is actually made of chemical compounds that include nitrogen.

Pure nitrogen is a non-poisonous gas. You cannot see it, smell it or taste it. At room temperature it does not react with other chemicals. But nitrogen can combine with other elements to make many important compounds.

▶ Liquid nitrogen being used to preserve bone marrow. Nitrogen gas becomes a liquid at around –196°C.

Nitrogen compounds

Ammonia is a compound of nitrogen and hydrogen. It is made in factories, and is used to make fertilizers, explosives, and rocket fuels. Nitrogen is also found in all kinds of other chemicals, including nitric acid, which is important in industry. Some of the main pollutants in vehicle exhausts are nitrogen oxides.

🔵 **key words**
- air
- amino acid
- ammonia
- gas
- nitrogen
- protein

In living things, nitrogen is combined with carbon, oxygen and hydrogen in a number of complicated chemicals called amino acids. Amino acids link together in different ways to make lots of even more complicated chemicals called proteins. The cells in your body are largely made of proteins, and proteins have many other important functions in all living things.

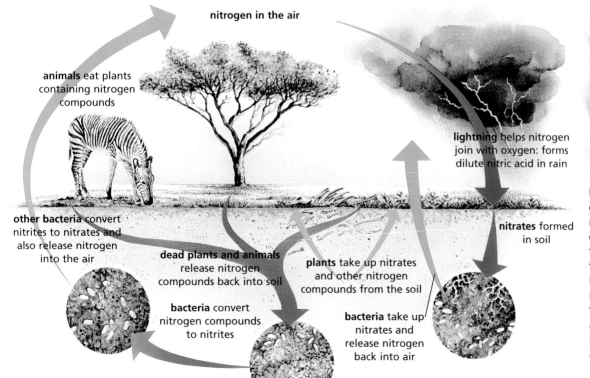

nitrogen in the air

animals eat plants containing nitrogen compounds

other bacteria convert nitrites to nitrates and also release nitrogen into the air

dead plants and animals release nitrogen compounds back into soil

bacteria convert nitrogen compounds to nitrites

plants take up nitrates and other nitrogen compounds from the soil

bacteria take up nitrates and release nitrogen back into air

lightning helps nitrogen join with oxygen: forms dilute nitric acid in rain

nitrates formed in soil

Because it is so unreactive, nitrogen is often added to food packages, such as crisp packets, to help keep the food fresh.

◀ The nitrogen cycle. Plants and animals can't get the nitrogen they need to make proteins directly from the air. In the nitrogen cycle, with the help of various kinds of microbe, nitrogen moves from the air into plants and animals and back again, helping to sustain life as it does so.

THE GAS OF LIFE

When you breathe in, about a fifth of the air that rushes into your lungs is oxygen. Without this oxygen we would die of suffocation. But scuba divers don't carry pure oxygen in their air tanks. Too much oxygen can be poisonous.

Pure oxygen is a gas. You cannot see it, smell it or taste it. As well as existing in its uncombined form in the atmosphere, oxygen is the commonest element in the rocks and minerals that make up the Earth's crust. Combined with hydrogen, oxygen makes water, which covers two-thirds of the surface of the Earth.

Combining with oxygen

When oxygen combines with other materials, the common process is called oxidation. When something burns, it is combining with the oxygen in the air. This process is called combustion. It is a kind of chemical reaction, and heat energy is given out. When pure hydrogen burns, it combines with oxygen to make water.

There isn't always a fire when oxygen combines with other elements. For example, when iron is exposed to the air, it slowly reacts with the oxygen to form iron oxide – rust.

Without plants to renew the oxygen supply in the air, we would soon run out of oxygen. The Amazon rainforest produces a fifth of all the oxygen made by plants.

oxygen   **ozone**

◀ Molecules of oxygen gas have two oxygen atoms, while the molecules of its bigger relative ozone have three.

Uses of oxygen

Oxygen is used in many important industrial processes – in steel-making, for example, and in the preparation of nitric and sulphuric acids. Oxygen compounds are used in the manufacture of materials such as plastics. Oxygen's power to burn, or oxidize, other materials is used in welding, explosives, rocket fuels, and even in treating sewage.

▲ In a fire, the material that is burning is actually combining with oxygen in the air.

Respiration

Most living things need oxygen – only some kinds of bacteria can live without it. We use oxygen to release energy from food. This process, called respiration, takes place in the cells of our bodies. Carbon dioxide and water are given out as the waste product of respiration. Land animals breathe in oxygen from the air, but fish have gills so they can extract (take) oxygen from water. Plants also need oxygen, but they produce more oxygen than they use.

Oxygen is a waste product of photosynthesis, the process by which plants make sugary food from carbon dioxide, sunlight and water.

Ozone

The oxygen gas we breathe is made of molecules containing two atoms of oxygen. But there is another kind of oxygen gas in which the molecules have three oxygen atoms. This gas is called ozone. Ozone is poisonous, but there is normally only a very small amount in the air we breathe.

However, polluting gases from car exhausts can react with sunlight to make ozone, causing some people to have breathing difficulties.

Ozone is, however, very important to us. High up in the Earth's atmosphere there is a thin layer of ozone, which protects us from the Sun's harmful ultraviolet radiation. This layer has been damaged by various man-made chemicals, including the CFCs (chlorofluorocarbons) that were used in aerosol sprays. Although CFCs are no longer so widely used, the ozone layer will take many years to recover.

key words

- combustion
- element
- oxidation
- oxygen
- ozone
- respiration

▲ High up in the atmosphere, the air is thinner and there is much less oxygen. At these great heights, fighter pilots and mountaineers need to breathe from bottles of oxygen.

▶ In an oxyacetylene torch, oxygen gas makes the acetylene fuel burn very fiercely. This produces enough heat to cut metals, or to weld pieces of metal together.

◀ Antoine Lavoisier (1743–1794)

THE DISCOVERY OF OXYGEN

Until the late 18th century, no one knew why things burned – although there were plenty of theories. Then, in 1772, the Swedish chemist Carl Wilhelm Scheele (1735–1804) discovered oxygen. But Scheele did not announce his discovery for several years – until after the British chemist Joseph Priestley announced in 1774 that he had discovered oxygen. However, it was left to the French chemist Antoine Lavoisier to realize that oxygen was an element, and that when things burn they are reacting with oxygen.

FIRE AND BRIMSTONE

If you were foolish enough to stand on the rim of a smoking volcano, you might well smell rotten eggs. The stink is a poisonous gas called hydrogen sulphide – a compound of sulphur and hydrogen. Sulphur is often found around volcanoes and hot springs. For this reason, people used to associate sulphur – or 'brimstone' as they called it – with the underworld and the devil.

Sulphur is a yellow non-metallic element, which is solid at room temperature. It can combine with most other elements. Although some of its compounds are poisonous, others are essential to life.

Pure sulphur

Pure sulphur has three basic forms, or allotropes. In two of them, the sulphur atoms are arranged regularly into crystal

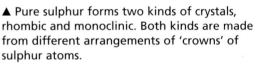

rhombic sulphur

'crown' of sulphur atom

monoclinic sulphur

▲ Pure sulphur forms two kinds of crystals, rhombic and monoclinic. Both kinds are made from different arrangements of 'crowns' of sulphur atoms.

key words

- allotrope
- crystal
- element
- sulphur

▼ Sulphur leaves beautifully coloured deposits around volcanic vents.

shapes. In rhombic sulphur the crystals are squat, while in monoclinic sulphur they are shaped like needles. The third allotrope is plastic sulphur, which forms when molten sulphur is poured into cold water. Plastic sulphur has no regular shape.

Sulphur is found in many parts of the world, deep underground. It is extracted by drilling a hole and pumping down extremely hot water. This melts the sulphur, which is then blasted to the surface by pressurized air.

Uses of sulphur

Sulphur is an ingredient in matches and gunpowder, and is used to harden rubber – a process called vulcanization. Sulphur is also the basis of many other chemicals, such as sulphuric acid, which is an important raw material in many industries. Some sulphur compounds are important medicines. Others are used by farmers to kill the fungi that attack crops.

When sulphur burns, it makes sulphur dioxide, a poisonous gas. This is produced by coal-fired power stations, and can form damaging acid rain. Sulphur dioxide does have its uses though – for example, as a preservative for jams and other foods.

SOFT METALS

Some metals, such as sodium and potassium, are so soft that you can cut them with a knife. They are also fiercely reactive – if you put a piece of sodium in water, it will shoot across the surface, fizzing violently. Such metals are never found naturally in their pure state, but they make many stable compounds. For example, common table salt is sodium chloride.

Sodium and potassium belong to a group of highly reactive metal elements. The other elements in the group are lithium, rubidium, caesium and francium. They are all soft, less dense than other metals, and have low boiling points.

Properties

These metals are arranged in a column in the periodic table of the elements, from the least reactive to the most reactive.

At the top is lithium. Lithium is silvery white, and is the least reactive. Sodium comes below lithium, and is also silvery white. Like potassium below it, sodium reacts rapidly with air and violently in water, so it has to be stored under oil. Below potassium is rubidium, which bursts into flames if exposed to air. Francium and caesium, the remaining members of the group, are even more reactive.

Uses

Some medicines contain lithium. It is also used in batteries for things like mobile phones and digital watches.

Both sodium and potassium are essential for all living things. Potassium fertilizers are added to soil to help crops grow. We get most of the sodium we need from common salt – although too much can be harmful. Lamps containing sodium vapour give off a yellowish-orange light, and are used for street lighting.

Caesium is a key element in a car's catalytic converter. It helps to turn some exhaust gases into less polluting compounds.

◀ In some countries with a hot climate, table salt (sodium chloride) is obtained by trapping sea water in shallow pans or lagoons. When the sea water evaporates, 'sea salt' is left behind.

▶ When water is dripped onto a piece of potassium, there is an explosive reaction.

key words
- caesium
- lithium
- potassium
- sodium

Sodium and potassium are used to colour fireworks. Sodium burns with a bright yellow flame, while potassium has a lilac flame.

THE STRENGTH IN YOUR BONES

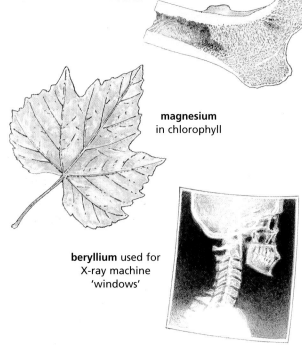

calcium essential in bones

magnesium in chlorophyll

beryllium used for X-ray machine 'windows'

What do sea shells, eggshells, milk, bones and teeth have in common? They all contain lots of calcium. Calcium is one of the commonest metals on Earth. It is found in many rocks – especially chalk, limestone and marble – in the form of calcium carbonate (a compound of calcium, carbon and oxygen).

Calcium belongs to a group of metallic elements that also includes beryllium, magnesium, strontium, barium and radium, which is radioactive.

▶ Some important functions of the calcium family of elements.

Properties and uses

These metals appear in the same column in the periodic table of the elements. They behave similarly to soft metals such as sodium, but are less reactive, harder and have higher melting points.

The least reactive member of the group is beryllium. It is used in alloys (mixtures of metals) to make cutting tools where it is important to avoid sparks. Minerals containing beryllium don't show up on

key words

- beryllium
- calcium
- element
- magnesium
- metal
- reactive

X-rays, and are used for the 'windows' of X-ray machines.

Magnesium is also used in alloys because it is strong and light. It is present in small quantities in living things. Most important of all, it is found in the chemical on which nearly all life on Earth depends – chlorophyll. Chlorophyll is a green pigment that can trap energy from sunlight. It is an important part of the process of photosynthesis, in which plants use the Sun's energy to make food from carbon dioxide and water.

Calcium is more reactive than beryllium or magnesium. When it reacts with air, a crust forms on its surface, stopping further reaction. Calcium is important in our diet, because it makes our bones strong. Calcium compounds have many uses, for example in the manufacture of cement, glass, fertilizers and explosives.

◀ These chalk cliffs are made from calcium carbonate. The chalk formed 80 million years ago as the shells of tiny sea creatures built up at the bottom of an ancient sea.

When you see a white flash in a firework display, that is magnesium burning. Red colours are produced by strontium compounds.

CHEMICAL NASTIES

On a misty wet evening, a car's headlights shine brightly through the dusk. The gases that allow the headlights to shine so brightly are part of a group called the halogens. Another halogen is used to keep swimming pools clean, and is half of common table salt.

Chlorine combines with sodium to make salt (sodium chloride). It is one of the halogens, a group of highly reactive non-metals that are all poisonous in their pure forms. They react with metals to make various kinds of salts ('halogen' means 'salt-making'). The other halogens are fluorine, bromine, iodine and astatine.

Properties and uses

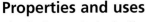

The halogen light bulbs used in car headlamps have a halogen gas, usually iodine or bromine, surrounding the light filament. Halogen bulbs are brighter and last much longer than ordinary light bulbs.

Fluorine forms very corrosive acids, such as hydrofluoric acid, which can be used to

◀ Chlorine and bromine were used in gas attacks in World War I (1914–1918). Soldiers had to wear gas masks to protect themselves.

▲ Chlorine is put in swimming pools to kill germs. Chlorine can react with sweat and urine in the water to make chemicals that sting your eyes – so many swimmers wear goggles.

key words

- bromine
- chlorine
- element
- fluorine
- halogen
- iodine
- non-metal
- reactive

etch (make patterns in) glass. Small amounts of fluoride compounds in toothpaste and drinking water help to prevent tooth decay.

Chlorine reacts with lots of other elements to make some very useful compounds such as PVC, a plastic used for pipes and waterproof fabrics. Compounds of chlorine, fluorine and carbon – the chlorofluorocarbons (CFCs) – were once widely used in aerosols. Then it was found that CFCs damaged the ozone layer, which protects us from the sun's harmful ultraviolet rays.

Iodine is a purplish black crystalline solid. At room temperature it sublimes (turns straight into a gas). It is found in small amounts in sea water, and in larger amounts in some seaweeds. The thyroid gland in your neck needs a tiny amount of iodine. It uses the iodine to make chemicals that keep your cells working properly. Iodine and its compounds are also used in medicine and photography.

In parts of the world where there is no iodine in the drinking water, some people used to suffer from goitre – a hugely swollen thryoid gland in the neck. Nowadays, small amounts of iodine compounds are added to table salt to prevent this.

NOBLE GASES

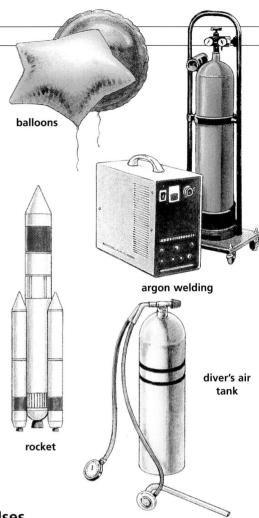

balloons

argon welding

rocket

diver's air tank

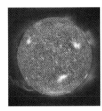

There is helium gas in the air you breathe – but only a tiny amount. In every 200,000 litres of air, there is only 1 litre of helium. But after hydrogen, helium is the commonest element in the Universe. Helium is created in the massive nuclear reactions that make the stars shine.

Helium is the lightest element, after hydrogen. It belongs to a group of unreactive elements called the noble gases. The other members of the group are neon, argon, krypton, xenon and radon. The noble gases are all present in tiny amounts in the Earth's atmosphere.

Properties

You cannot see or smell the noble gases. Scientists used to think that none of them ever reacted with any other elements, and as result they were called the 'inert gases'. However, chemists have now made compounds of xenon, krypton, and radon, so the name of the group has been changed to the 'noble' gases.

▶ Helium has many uses. It is so light that it is used to fill airships and balloons. It is also used to pressurize the hydrogen fuel in rockets, and the air in divers' air tanks. Argon welding is used to join pieces of aluminium or stainless steel.

 key words

- argon
- helium
- krypton
- neon
- radon

Uses

Apart from radon, which is radioactive, the noble gases are used in lighting. When a glass tube is filled with a noble gas and an electrical charge passes through it, the gas glows. Neon glows orange-red, for example, while krypton glows bluish-white.

The noble gases are also used to provide an unreactive atmosphere for certain processes such as welding metals.

The noble gases have very low boiling points, and are used to study matter at low temperatures. Liquid helium is the coldest substance – the gas only becomes liquid at −268.9°C.

Helium was discovered in 1868 when scientists studied light coming from the Sun. They named the new element after helios, the Greek word for the Sun.

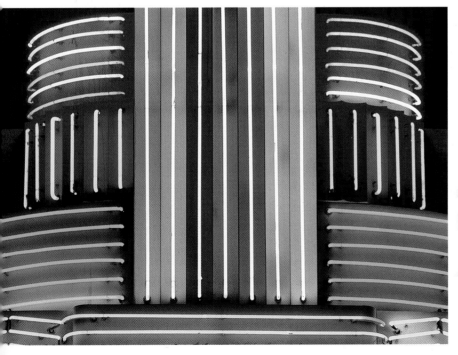

◀ This lighting display uses glass tubes filled with noble gases, which glow with different colours when an electrical charge passes through them.

CHEMISTRY IN ACTION

Chemistry doesn't just happen in scientific laboratories. Chemical reactions are going on all around you. For example, rusting, burning, cooking and breathing all involve chemical reactions.

A chemical reaction is a process in which a substance is changed chemically when it interacts with another substance. In the course of the reaction, chemical bonds between the atoms are made or broken. The substances you start with at the beginning of the reaction are called the reactants. The results of a reaction are new substances, the products. You can reverse some kinds of chemical reaction, but not others.

▶ Firework displays involve very fast, explosive chemical reactions. Different substances added to the gunpowder make the colours. Copper compounds, for example, give blue colours, while sodium compounds give yellow.

Reactions all around us

When iron rusts, it is slowly reacting with oxygen in the air. The product is iron oxide (rust). Iron oxide is a reddish, crumbly solid – very different from either iron (a strong grey metal) or oxygen (an invisible gas).

Lots of different reactions go on in cooking. When you fry or boil an egg, for example, the clear sludgy stuff round the yolk turns firm and white. A chemical reaction has taken place.

A whole series of complicated chemical reactions take place after we breathe in oxygen. One of the products is carbon dioxide gas, which we breathe out. There are many other reactions going on all the time inside us, involving thousands of different biological chemicals.

Chemical reactions are very important in many industries. They are used to make a huge range of products, from fertilizers and explosives to cleaning fluids and dyes. Some industries use living things as

◀ The iron in the metal bodies of old cars slowly reacts with oxygen in the air to make iron oxide – better known as rust.

miniature chemical factories. For example, yeast (a kind of microscopic fungus) helps to make bread and beer. Scientists now use bacteria to help make some medicines and even plastics.

Using and giving out energy

All chemical reactions use or give out energy – usually in the form of heat. Reactions that produce more energy than they take in include combustion (burning) reactions. When a substance burns, it is actually reacting with oxygen and giving off heat.

Reactions that take in more energy than they give out include the process used by plants to make their own food. Plants use the energy from sunlight to change carbon dioxide and water into glucose (a type of sugar) and oxygen.

The energy involved in reactions isn't always in the form of heat. Reactions where there are flames also give off energy in the form of light. Even more violent reactions, such as explosions, give off sound energy as well. Similarly, some reactions may be started by energy from electricity, light or sound – even by a blow from a hammer.

▲ The light from these fireflies is produced by a chemical reaction in the bodies of the insects.

key words

- catalyst
- combustion
- energy
- molecule
- product
- reactant

Some reactions work better if a substance called a catalyst is present. A catalyst helps the reaction to take place, but the catalyst itself does not change.

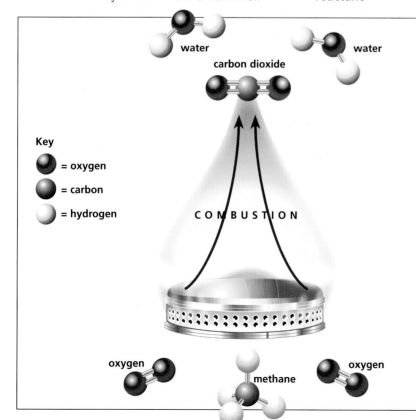

Key
- ● = oxygen
- ● = carbon
- ○ = hydrogen

water

carbon dioxide

water

COMBUSTION

oxygen

oxygen

methane

ANATOMY OF A REACTION

When methane burns on the top of a gas cooker, it is reacting with oxygen in the air to form carbon dioxide and water vapour. This chemical reaction can be written as an equation. The equation is a shorthand description of what happens in the reaction.

$$CH_4 + 2O_2 \rightarrow CO_2 + 2H_2O$$

The chemical symbols indicate the different substances involved in the reaction. Methane is made up of carbon atoms each linked to four hydrogen atoms (CH_4). Carbon dioxide is a carbon atom linked to two oxygen atoms (CO_2). Water is made up of oxygen atoms joined to two hydrogen atoms (H_2O), and oxygen gas is pairs of oxygen atoms (O_2). Burning is one example of a very common type of chemical reaction involving oxidation. Rust formation is another example: iron reacts with oxygen in the air to form rust. And the process by which the body breaks down food to get energy is a whole series of oxidation reactions.

BURNING BRIGHT

OLD IDEAS

In the ancient world, people believed that all things were made of four basic elements: fire, air, water, and earth. Later, scientists thought flammable (burnable) materials must contain a mysterious substance called 'phlogiston', which escaped when the material was burned, leaving ash behind. Just over 200 years ago, the French chemist Antoine Lavoisier showed that combustion is actually a chemical reaction between a fuel and a newly discovered gas – oxygen.

Humans first learnt how to tame fire about a million and a half years ago. They used it to warm themselves, to cook food and to frighten off wild animals. Later, our ancestors discovered how to use fire for baking clay and making metals.

Fire is a collection of very fast chemical reactions. These reactions – called combustion – give out lots of energy in the form of heat, light and sound.

When a substance burns, it is reacting fiercely with oxygen in the air. Combustion is a kind of oxidation reaction. During the reaction, each molecule (tiny particle) of the substance is torn apart to combine with oxygen, releasing the energy that held the molecule together.

Burning fuels

Fire is the quickest and simplest way to release energy from fuels. Energy is stored in fuels as chemical energy. The energy released can cook food, power cars and generate electricity.

◀ In every flame, complex chemical reactions are taking place. Air currents cause a candle flame to be teardrop-shaped. They also carry soot to the flame's tip, making it yellow.

The commonest fuels are hydrocarbons – materials such as coal, gas and oil, which contain compounds of carbon and hydrogen. When you burn hydrocarbon fuels, carbon dioxide and water are released as waste. If there is not enough oxygen, however, the fire will release other products, such as carbon monoxide and particles of partly burnt fuel (smoke), which pollute the atmosphere.

◀ In nature, fires are usually started when lightning strikes dry vegetation. Some kinds of forests and grasslands actually need regular fires to flourish.

key words

- combustion
- energy
- fire
- fuel
- oxidation

VINEGAR AND BLEACH

If you taste something sour, like lemon juice, vinegar or milk that's gone off, your tongue is detecting the acid in these liquids. Your body can detect acids in other ways too – when you get stung by an ant or a nettle, it is the acid in their stings that makes it hurt.

Lemon juice and vinegar are weak acids. Strong acids are much too dangerous to taste or touch. They are corrosive, which means that they can eat into skin, wood, cloth and other materials.

The chemical opposite of an acid is an alkali. Many alkalis, such as bleach and oven-cleaner, can be just as corrosive as strong acids.

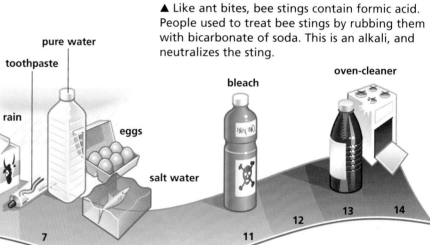

▲ Like ant bites, bee stings contain formic acid. People used to treat bee stings by rubbing them with bicarbonate of soda. This is an alkali, and neutralizes the sting.

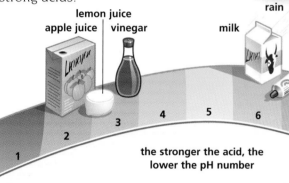

apple juice · lemon juice · vinegar · rain · toothpaste · pure water · milk · eggs · salt water · bleach · oven-cleaner

1 2 3 4 5 6 7 8 9 10 11 12 13 14

the stronger the acid, the lower the pH number

the stronger the alkali, the higher the pH number

▲ Scientists use the pH scale to measure how acid or alkali something is. Neutral substances, such as pure water, have a pH of 7.

◀ Cola drinks contain phosphoric acid to give them flavour. But the acid combines with the sugar in the drink to rot your teeth.

Properties

Acids form a big group of chemicals that all behave in similar ways. Acids all contain hydrogen, and when they react with metals such as iron and zinc, they give off hydrogen gas. When acids touch a special paper, called litmus paper, they turn it red.

Alkalis are part of a group of chemicals called bases: alkalis are bases that dissolve in water. Many alkalis have a bitter taste and feel soapy. But do not try to taste or touch an alkali – you will be badly burned. Alkalis all contain hydroxide (hydrogen joined to oxygen), and turn litmus paper blue.

Scientists measure the strength of acids and alkalis on a scale of numbers called the pH scale. The scale ranges from 14 (the strongest alkali) to 0 (the strongest acids).

Mixing acids and alkalis

When an acid meets an alkali, both are changed – they are neutralized. What happens is that the hydrogen from the acid joins the hydroxide from the alkali to make water (a molecule of water has two hydrogen atoms and one oxygen atom). The parts of the acid and alkali left behind make a salt. For example, when hydrochloric acid reacts with sodium hydroxide (an alkali), the result is water and sodium chloride – common table salt.

Uses

Lots of acids occur in nature, and are found inside your body. For example, your stomach produces hydrochloric acid to help digest your food. DNA, the complicated chemical that stores your genetic code, is deoxyribonucleic acid.

Strong acids, especially sulphuric acid, are used in factories to make fertilizers, explosives, plastics, synthetic fabrics, paints, dyes, medicines, detergents, and many other chemicals.

Weak alkalis such as milk of magnesia are good for indigestion caused by too much acid in the stomach. They work by neutralizing the acid.

▶ This portrait by the Dutch artist Rembrandt is an etching. Etching is a way of printing pictures that uses acid. The artist draws lines with a steel needle on a copper plate covered in acid-resistant material. The plate then goes into a bath of acid, which bites into the copper where the artist has drawn the lines. The coating is then removed, and the plate is ready to make prints.

Strong alkalis such as sodium hydroxide (caustic soda) feel slippery to touch, because when they react with oils on your skin they form a kind of human soap – don't try this, it will burn your skin. Because sodium hydroxide solution dissolves fats, it is used to clear blocked drains and in oven cleaners.

In industry, alkalis are used in the manufacture of soap, glass, paper and textiles, and in the refining of crude oil.

🔵 **key words**
- acid
- alkali
- neutralization
- salt

(a) make a water-tight 'volcano' out of plasticine or clay and place it on a plate

(b) mix together a few drops of red food colouring, a squirt of washing-up liquid and a tablespoon of baking powder

(c) pour the mixture into the volcano

(d) add about a tablespoon of vinegar

(e) the volcano erupts

◀ This 'volcano' works using a neutralization reaction. The vinegar (acid) and baking powder (bicarbonate of soda – an alkali) react together to form a neutral chemical (a salt), water and the gas carbon dioxide. It is the gas that makes the 'volcano' erupt.

WHEN ACIDS MEET ALKALIS

Common salt – the white powdery stuff you sprinkle on your chips – is the most widely used mineral in the world. But common salt is just one of a large number of chemical substances called salts.

Most salts are crystalline solids that can dissolve in water. They generally melt only at high temperatures – common salt becomes a liquid at 801 °C.

Salts are made up of tiny, electrically charged atoms, or ions. Salts usually consist of a metal ion (this has a positive charge) and a non-metal ion (this is negatively charged). For example, common salt is sodium chloride – sodium ions (metal) and chloride ions (non-metal).

key words
- acid
- alkali
- crystal
- metal
- non-metal

Making salts
Salts are the result of mixing two other kinds of chemical, acids and alkalis. For example, if you mix hydrochloric acid and sodium hydroxide (also known as caustic

▼ A crystal of common salt seen through a microscope.

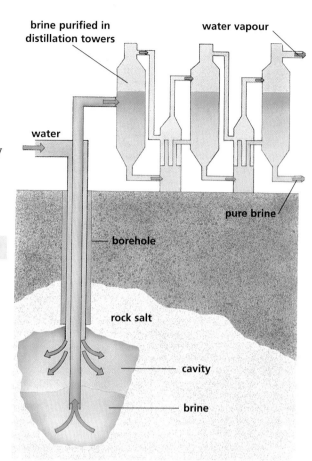

▲ Salt can be mined by a process called solution mining. A borehole is drilled into the rock salt and two pipes are inserted, one inside the other. Water is pumped in through the outer pipe, and dissolves the rock to make brine. The brine is pushed out of the ground through the inner pipe.

soda, an alkali), you get sodium chloride and water.

Most common salt comes from deposits deep underground. Salt is also obtained from the sea in hot countries. Sea water is trapped in shallow pools, and the water evaporates leaving salt crystals.

Uses of salts
Common salt has been used for thousands of years to preserve and flavour foods. It is used in the manufacture of dyes, paper, pottery, leather, medicines and chemicals. Other salts also have a huge range of uses. For example, copper sulphate is used in sprays to kill fungi attacking crops. Various salts containing silver are light-sensitive and are used to coat photographic film. Many other salts are used in medicine and in all kinds of industries.

CHEMICAL CHAINS

The tiny fibres in this paper, the starch in the bread you eat and the muscles you're using to hold this book all have one thing in common. It's the same thing that links car windscreens, nylon thread and the outsides of telephones and ballpoint pens.

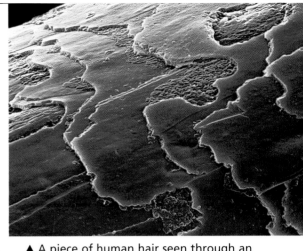

▲ A piece of human hair seen through an electron microscope. Hair is made of a protein called keratin. All proteins, the building blocks of living things, are polymers.

All these things are made of polymers. Polymers are a special kind of molecule. All chemical compounds (substances) are made of molecules. Many molecules are small and simple, but a polymer forms a long chain made up of thousands of repeating building blocks, called monomers (poly- means 'many' and mono- means 'single').

▼ PVC (polyvinyl chloride) is a common polymer used to make water pipes, window frames, flooring and many other products. The repeating unit (monomer) in PVC is vinyl chloride.

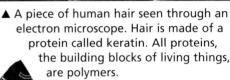

◀ The high-performance clothing and equipment used by these climbers in the Himalayas is nearly all made from synthetic polymers.

Proteins – the complicated chemicals that make up your muscles and much of the rest of your body – are all polymers. They are made from chains of simpler chemicals called amino acids.

DNA, the molecule that stores your genetic code in every cell of your body, is also a polymer. Rubber is another natural polymer.

Artificial polymers

All plastics, from nylon to PVC, are polymers. The first plastic was celluloid, made in 1869 from the cellulose in cotton fibres. In 1909 another plastic, bakelite, was made by joining up smaller molecules to make a big polymer molecule.

Since then, a huge range of artificial polymers has been made. They have all kinds of uses because they can be shaped, they are strong and lightweight, and they can be made with many different properties.

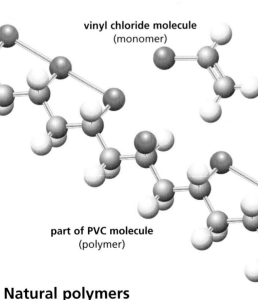

vinyl chloride molecule
(monomer)

part of PVC molecule
(polymer)

key words
- cellulose
- molecule
- monomer
- plastic
- protein
- starch

Natural polymers

In nature, polymers are found in many carbohydrates, such as starch and cellulose. Cellulose is the fibrous material in plants. It is made up of many units of glucose (a simple sugar).

WHAT'S IT MADE OF?

If you have a glass of salty water and a glass of sugary water, how do you tell which is which? The easiest way is to taste them. Your tongue is actually a very clever chemical laboratory. But if you don't know what a liquid is, it is best not to taste it. It might be poisonous!

Finding out what things are made of is called chemical analysis. Scientists have developed a whole range of tests to help them do this.

Chemical analysis is used to test for all kinds of things. Chemists test drinking water to see if it has been polluted with dangerous chemicals. In hospitals, biochemists test samples of blood, saliva and urine from patients. They are looking for chemicals that show someone has a particular illness. Forensic chemists help the police, for example, by checking for poison in the body of a murder victim.

▼ You can spot different metals in chemical compounds by seeing what colour flames they produce. Here are the flames produced by sodium (on the left), strontium (middle) and boric acid (which contains the metal boron).

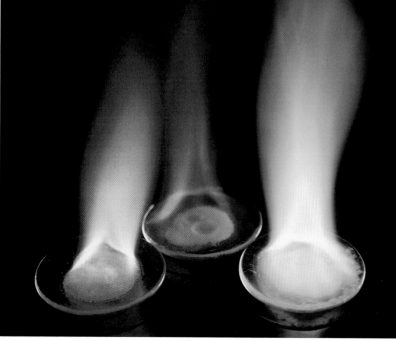

Flame and fire

One of the simplest chemical tests is to check for the presence of a metal in a sample. All you need to do is burn a tiny amount of the sample and look at the colour of the flame. Different metals burn with different colours. For example, calcium has an orange-red flame, while potassium burns lilac.

▲ Scientists testing the chemicals in a hot spring in Yellowstone National Park, USA.

Burning is also used to analyse organic compounds (chemicals containing carbon). The method involves burning a sample of the compound until it breaks down into its individual elements (basic substances). Scientists can then measure how much there is of each of the common elements in organic compounds – carbon, hydrogen, oxygen and nitrogen.

Changing colours

Chemists use various substances to check for the presence of particular chemicals. These substances, called indicators, change colour if the chemical is present. Iodine in solution has a purplish colour, but if you put a drop onto something containing starch, the solution will turn black. Another important indicator is special paper called litmus paper. It turns red if touched by an acid, and blue if touched by an alkali (the chemical opposite of an acid).

Another technique using colour is called chromatography. A simple experiment using chromatography shows what's in the coloured coatings of some sweets. Dissolve the coating of the sweet in a little bit of water. Then put a drop of the solution onto blotting paper. You will see that there are actually different colours, each one spreading out from the drop at a different speed. You are left with a series of coloured rings, one for each of the chemicals in the coating of the sweet.

Using spectra

White light is actually made up of different colours, called the spectrum. If you shine white light through a thin slice of material, the light will be broken up into different colours in a particular way. Scientists can use this to spot particular substances or elements. This technique is called spectroscopy. Other forms of radiation,

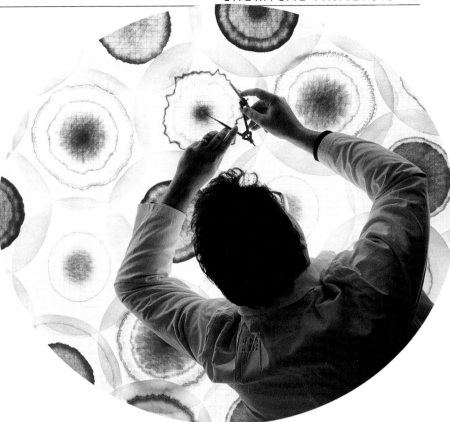

▲ Chromatography is used in laboratories to separate and analyse some substances. Here a scientist measures the results for different industrial dyes.

including infrared, ultraviolet and X-rays, can also be used this way.

Mass spectrometry is one of the most powerful ways of analysing many kinds of chemical. In this technique, a substance is broken up into charged fragments, and electric and magnetic fields are used to measure the mass (weight) of each fragment. Different compounds have their own characteristic mass spectrum, which can be used to identify them.

DNA FINGERPRINTING
DNA is the genetic material in the cells of all living things. Each individual has a virtually unique set of DNA (only clones or identical twins have the same DNA). DNA fingerprinting is a way of identifying the differences between people's DNA. It is used to identify criminals and to find out how closely people are related. It is also used to study breeding in wild animals.

The technique works by breaking up the long DNA molecule into fragments. Certain 'core' fragments are then tagged with radioactivity and separated using a technique called electrophoresis. The result is a pattern of bands that is different for each individual. Similarities between patterns can show how closely related individuals are.

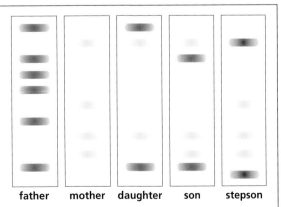

father   mother   daughter   son   stepson

The patterns shown here are for a family (the colours have been added to help the explanation). Two of the children have a mixture of the mother's and the father's DNA fingerprints. The third child has a different father (red).

GLOSSARY

This glossary gives simple explanations of difficult or specialist words that readers might be unfamiliar with. Words in *italic* have their own glossary entry.

allotrope A different form of the same *element*. Graphite, charcoal and diamond are all allotropes of carbon.

amorphous Having no definite form or structure; a non-crystalline material.

atom The smallest particle of an *element*, made up of a tiny central *nucleus* surrounded by a cloud of fast-moving *electrons*.

carbohydrate A natural sugar-like compound made from the *elements* carbon, hydrogen and oxygen.

catalyst A chemical used to help bring about or speed up a chemical *reaction*, but which is not actually changed itself in the process.

compound A substance made of two or more different *elements* bonded together.

condensation The process by which a gas turns into a liquid.

conductor A substance, such as a metal, that allows an electric *current* to flow through it.

crystal A solid material with *atoms* arranged in a geometric pattern. All minerals form crystals.

current A measure of the rate at which electric charge (*electrons*) flows around an electric circuit.

density A measure of the amount (*mass*) of a material in a particular volume. The metal lead, for instance, has a high density, because its mass is packed into a small volume.

ductile Describing a material (a metal) that can be drawn into thin wires without breaking.

electricity A form of energy carried by certain particles of matter (*electrons* and *protons*), used for lighting and heating and for making machines work.

electron A tiny negatively charged particle that orbits the *nucleus* of an *atom*.

element A substance that is made of only one kind of *atom*. Elements cannot be broken down into other substances.

evaporation The process by which a liquid turns into a gas.

fission The process of splitting an *atom* to release nuclear energy.

fusion The process of combining the *nuclei* of *atoms* to release energy.

gravity The force that attracts two objects. Earth's gravity keeps everything on Earth from floating out into space.

insulator A substance, such as rubber, that blocks the flow of electric *current*.

isotope A different form of the same *element*, with fewer or more *neutrons* in its *nucleus* but the same number of *protons*.

malleable Describing a material (a metal) that can be hammered into shape without cracking.

mass The amount of material (solid, liquid or gas) that something contains.

molecule A group of two or more *atoms* bonded to each other.

neutron A basic particle found in the *nucleus* of an *atom*, which has no electrical charge.

nucleus The central part of an *atom*, which usually consists of *protons* and *neutrons*.

pressure The amount of force being applied (for example, by a gas or liquid) over a given area.

proton One of the basic particles found in the *nucleus* of an *atom*. Protons have a positive electric charge.

radiation Energy given off as waves or tiny particles. Heat, light and sound are different types of radiation.

radioactive Having *atoms* that break up and send out particles or rays of energy (*radiation*), which produce electrical and chemical effects and penetrate things. Uranium is a highly radioactive material.

reaction A chemical change in which one or more *elements* form new *compounds*.

viscosity A measure of how much a fluid resists flowing. Treacle is thick, sticky and viscous – it does not pour easily.

weight The force with which everything presses down on the ground, water or air beneath it, as a result of *gravity*.

INDEX

Page numbers in **bold** mean that this is where you will find the most information on that subject. If both a heading and a page number are in bold, there is an article with that title. A page number in *italic* means that there is a picture of that subject. There may also be other information about the subject on the same page.

Acknowledgements

Key
t = top; c = centre; b = bottom; r = right; l = left; back = background; fore = foreground

Artwork
D'Achille, Gino: 22 tr; 31 bl. **Franklin, Mark:** 5 tl; 8 tr; 10 cr; 11 bl. **Full Steam Ahead:** 6 tr; 22–23 main; 23 tr; 45 b. **Gecko Ltd.:** 19 tr. **Hincks, Gary:** 28 bl; 29 bl. **Hook, Richard:** 39 tl. **Jakeway, Rob:** 7 b; 9 bl; 13 b; 15 tl; 16 tr; 16 br; 17 bl; 20 tr; 20 c; 21 b; 22 tl; 26 bl; 27 bl; 30 br; 32 tr; 38 bl; 43 bl. **Oxford Illustrators:** 14 bl. **Parsley, Helen:** 27 tl; 41 b. **Saunders, Michael:** 29 tl; 42 tr. **Smith, Guy:** 13 tr. **Sneddon, James:** 4 b; 18 cr; 40 c. **Visscher, Peter:** 4 tl; 6 tl; 7 tl; 8 tl; 9 tl; 10 tl; 11 tl; 12 tl; 14 tl; 17 tl; 20 tl; 24 tl; 24–25 bc; 30 tl; 32 tl; 33 tl; 34 tl; 35 tl; 36 tl; 38 tl; 40 tl; 42 tl; 43 tl; 44 tl; 48 tl.

Photos
The publishers would like to thank the following for permission to use their photographs.

Allsport: 28 tr (Nick Wilson); 35 tr (Donald Miralle). **Art Archive, The:** 21 tr (Biblioteca Bertoliana Vicenza/Dagli Orti). **Burges, Sean:** 24 bl. **Chris Bonington Picture Library:** 43 c. **Corbis:** 9 cr (Jim Sugar Photography); 12 bl (Paul A. Souders); 17 tr (Hulton-Deutsch Collection); 18 bl; 27 tr (W. Perry Conway); 29 tr (Leif Skoogfors); 30–31 c (Georgia Lowell); 31 tr (George Hall); 35 bl; 41 tr (Historical Picture Archive); 44–45 c (Ted Spiegel). **Goodyear:** 10 bl. **NASA:** 4 tr (Jeff Hester (Arizona State University)); 26 tl (Hubble Heritage Team (AURA/STScI)); 26 tr.

Oxford Scientific Films: 11 cr (John Downer); 38 tr (Satoshi Kuribayashi); 40 tr (Scott Camazine/K. Visscher); 40 bl (Haddon Davies). **Science Photo Library:** 5 br (Simon Fraser); 6 bl (David Nunuk); 7 tr (Arnold Fisher); 8 bl (Hermann Eisenbeiss); 12 tr (Alex Bartel); 12–13 c (Klaus Guldbrandsen); 14 tr (Philippe Plailly); 15 br (David Parker); 15 c (Peter Fowler); 15 tl (David Parker); 16 cl (CERN); 19 br (Novosti); 20 bl (Pascal Goetgheluck); 24 tr (Alfred Pasieka); 25 tr (Chris Knapton); 28 cr (Jan Hinsch); 32 bl (Bernhard Edmaier); 33 br (Charles D. Winters); 33 c (Bob Edwards); 34 bl (Martin Bond); 36 bl (Spencer Grant); 37 br (John Mead); 38 cr (Françoise Sauze); 39 bl (Scott Camazine/K. Visscher); 42 bl (Alfred Pasieka); 43 tr (David Scharf); 44 bl (Charles D. Winters); 45 tr (Geoff Tompkinson). **SOHO/EIT consortium** (SOHO is a project of international cooperation between ESA and NASA): 36 tr.